Our selection of the city's best places to eat, drink and experience:

⊙ **Sights**

✕ **Eating**

☐ **Drinking**

★ **Entertainment**

🔒 **Shopping**

These symbols give you the vital information for each listing:

📞	Telephone Numbers	👪	Family-Friendly
🕐	Opening Hours	🐾	Pet-Friendly
🅿	Parking	🚌	Bus
🚭	Nonsmoking	🚢	Ferry
@	Internet Access	Ⓜ	Metro
🛜	Wi-Fi Access	Ⓢ	Subway
🥗	Vegetarian Selection	🚋	Tram
📖	English-Language Menu	🚆	Train

Find each listing quickly on maps for each neighbourhood:

Bar Hemingway

16 ☐ Map p233, B2

Legend has it that Hemi
self, wielding a machine
erate this timber-pan
ered bar during
showpiece is a
en by Papa ar
town. Dress
s.com; Hôtel Rit
🕐 6.30pm-2a

Lonely Planet's Los Angeles

Lonely Planet Pocket Guides are designed to get you straight to the heart of the city.

Inside you'll find all the must-see sights, plus tips to make your visit to each one really memorable. We've split the city into easy-to-navigate neighborhoods and provided clear maps so you'll find your way around with ease. Our expert authors have searched out the best of the city: walks, food, nightlife and shopping, to name a few. Because you want to explore, our 'Local Life' pages will take you to some of the most exciting areas to experience the real Los Angeles.

And of course you'll find all the practical tips you need for a smooth trip: itineraries for short visits, how to get around, and how much to tip the guy who serves you a drink at the end of a long day's exploration.

It's your guarantee of a really great experience.

Our Promise

You can trust our travel information because Lonely Planet authors visit the places we write about, each and every edition. We never accept freebies for positive coverage, so you can rely on us to tell it like it is.

 KT-421-974

The Best of Los Angeles 151

Los Angeles' Best Walks

Los Angeles' Best...

Survival Guide 169

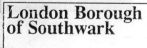

QuickStart Guide

Welcome to Los Angeles

LA runs deeper than her blonde beaches and celebrified hills would have you believe. She's a beacon for small-town dreamers, an open-minded angel best defined by simple, life-affirming moments – a cracked-ice, jazz-age cocktail on Beverly Blvd, or a hike high into the Hollywood Hills sagebrush. And her night music. There is always night music.

You are the Star mural by Thomas Suriya, Hollywood Blvd

WITOLD SKRYPCZAK/LONELY PLANET IMAGES ©

Los Angeles Top Sights

Hollywood Boulevard & the Walk of Fame (p24)

In LA stars are more visible on-screen, in high-end restaurants and embedded in this speckled sidewalk than they are in the hazy night sky.

DAVID PEEVERS/LONELY PLANET IMAGES ©

Griffith Observatory & Hollywood Sign (p42)

Two iconic sights dominate the Hollywood Hills ridgeline. One is a stylish window onto the universe. The other needs no introduction.

La Brea Tar Pits & Page Museum (p72)

Deep below Wilshire Blvd is a gooey archaeological treasure trove of crude oil, tusks and bones, where thousands of ice-age critters met their maker between 40,000 and 10,000 years ago.

LACMA (p74)

LACMA is not just LA's premier museum, it's a vortex of art, jazz, film and culture not to be missed. (*Urban Light* by Chris Burden)

Santa Monica Pier & Beach (p90)

Santa Monica's one essential landmark is absolutely unmissable and best experienced at its very edge, where waves lap against the barnacled pylons.

Venice Boardwalk (p104)

There is only one Venice Beach, and the boardwalk is where she lets her freak flag fly. Be prepared to encounter almost anything you can imagine.

Walt Disney Concert Hall (p120)

Where brilliant music meets virtuoso architecture. Take a bow, Mr Gehry. You make the LA Philharmonic look good.

Universal Studios (p138)

The magic of movie-making gets its due at ever-popular Universal, one of the world's oldest continuously operating movie studios and theme parks.

Disneyland & Disney California Adventure (p146)

The Happiest Place on Earth is an 'imagineered' utopia where both staff and visitors are forever upbeat, the thrills are wholesome and there's a parade every day.

Malibu (p100)

A moneyed but still laid-back beach town, Malibu rambles along the Pacific Coast Hwy for 27 gorgeous miles blessed with stunning coastal mountains, pristine coves and epic waves.

Getty Center (p68)

The Getty Center presents triple delights: a stellar art collection (Renaissance to David Hockney), Richard Meier's cutting-edge architecture, and truly captivating seasonal gardens.

Mulholland Drive (p38)

If you found David Lynch's *Mulholland Drive* a tad bizarre, perhaps a drive along this legendary road that winds through the Santa Monica Mountains, delivering iconic views at each bend, will clarify things.

Los Angeles Local Life

Insider tips to help you find the real city

LA is more a neighborhood quilt than a traditional metropolis, so in your haste to explore LA's best-known barrios, don't forget to sample her out-of-the-way corners, too.

Shopping the Fashion District (p122)

▶ Sample sales
▶ Santee Alley

Bargain hunters love this frantic 100-block warren of fashion. Deals are plentiful, but the district's size and immense selection can be as bewildering as the juxtaposition of sassy fashionistas wandering among drunks with neck tattoos and a perma-haze.

Echo Park (p52)

▶ Sage & Kind Kreme
▶ Echo & Echoplex

Echo Park is one of LA's old-school, working-class, multi-ethnic neighborhoods, and home to an emerging and intriguing creative subculture.

Culver City (p86)

▶ Akasha

A few years ago Culver City bloomed from its bland, semisuburban studio-town roots into a stylish yet unpretentious destination for fans of art, culture and food.

Long Beach (p116)

▶ Aquarium of the Pacific
▶ Belmont Shore

Long Beach has come a long way since its working-class oil and navy days. Over the past decade or so, LA's southernmost seaside town has quietly reinvented its gritty downtown.

Manhattan Beach (p114)

▶ MB Post
▶ Ercole's

If you love laid-back beach towns complete with string bikinis, bronzed surfers and a touch of class, you'll love it here.

Pasadena (p134)

▶ Norton Simon Museum
▶ Red White & Bluezz

Here is a robust community steeped in Americana, with a preppy old soul, a historical perspective and an appreciation for art and jazz.

Aquarium of the Pacific (p117), Long Beach

Volleyball game, Manhattan Beach (p114)

Other great places to experience the city like a local:

Dodger Stadium (p53)

Tiara Café (p123)

Downtown Art Walks (p123)

Uncle Bill's Pancake House (p115)

I Am 8 Bit (p53)

Ford's Filling Station (p87)

Kirk Douglas Theatre (p87)

Mohawk Bend (p53)

Market (p123)

Los Angeles Day Planner

Day One

Begin your day in West Hollywood with a quick breakfast at **Joan's on Third** (p80) before perusing the boutiques on Beverly Blvd, Melrose Pl and Melrose Ave. Explore **Hollywood Blvd** (p24) and the **Walk of Fame** (p24), and grab lunch at the **Loteria Grill** (p29).

After a quick peek in **Amoeba Music** (p36) for some road tunes, take **Mulholland Dr** (p38) west and stop at the **Getty Center** (p68), where you can indulge your cultural cravings and glimpse some epic views. Then keep pushing west to the **Venice Boardwalk** (p104) for sunset.

After a sunset beach stroll, find your way to Venice's trendy **Abbot Kinney** (p107) shopping district, where you can peer into the **Gebert Gallery** (p112) and hit **Gjelina** (p107) for a fantastic dinner of creative small plates and thin-crust pizza. If it's a **First Friday** (p107) of the month, join the art walkers. Otherwise, double back to Hollywood for rum and burlesque at **La Descarga** (p31).

Day Two

Day two is all about the east side, so start with breakfast downtown at **$.05 Diner** (p129) before hitting the **Grammy Museum** (p126) at LA Live for some harmonic time-travel. Then it's on to **MOCA** (p126), where you may lose yourself in color and form, before lunch at **Bottega Louie** (p128).

After a brief glimpse of the **Robert Reynolds Gallery** (p133), make your way through **Echo Park** (p52) and don't forget to pause at **Spitfire Girl** (p50) for a fun shop. Then take another long browse among the hipster boutiques of Silver Lake's Sunset Blvd strip. And don't miss **Matrushka Construction** (p50).

Continue shopping on trendy Hillhurst Ave, where a stopover at the Big Bar at **Alcove** (p47) is a must. If you are excessively hungry (or thirsty), you can also grab a meal here, or duck into nearby **Sushi Ike** (p29) for spectacular sushi in divey environs before catching a show at the **Upright Citizens Brigade** (p32).

Short on time?
We've arranged LA's must-sees into these day-by-day itineraries to make sure you
see the very best of the city in the time you have available.

Day Three

☀ It's time to soak up the sun, sand
and the Pacific blue, so fuel up with
a proper American breakfast at **Uncle
Bill's Pancake House** (p115) in Manhattan Beach before making your way up the
coast and onto the **Venice Boardwalk**
(p104). The **Santa Monica Pier** (p90)
should be coming into view, so take a picture among the anglers before hitting the
Santa Monica farmers markets (p96)
and the **Blue Plate Oysterette** (p94) for
a light, briny midday snack.

☀ Hit **Huckleberry** (p94) for coffee
and a pastry before perusing Main
St and the **Third Street Promenade**
(p98). Take a stroll along **Santa Monica
Beach** (p90), then continue up the coast
and into Malibu, where you can watch the
sun set beyond Point Dume at **Westward**
(p101) or **El Matador State Beach** (p101).

☽ Now that the sun has dropped, it's
time to loop south back into Santa
Monica, where you can get a superb meal
at **Rustic Canyon** (p94) before stopping
for a drink at **Basement Tavern** (p96).

Day Four

☀ Day four is about filling the gaps,
so after grazing at **Hugo's** (p60)
for an industry breakfast, take your
time and appreciate the greatness that
is **LACMA** (p74). It'll take some time
to explore all of the many galleries and
installations on offer here, so if the kids
get bored, consider a diversion to the **La
Brea Tar Pits** (p72) and **Page Museum**
(p72) before lunching at the original
Farmers Market (p81).

☀ Hit **Rodeo Dr** (p65) for a blast of
Beverly Hills bling before exploring
the (much!) less sophisticated jumble
that is **Melrose Ave** (p67), and then take
a sunset hike up **Runyon Canyon** (p39).

☽ After dark, take a long overdue
driving tour of the set-piece Sunset Strip, then head down to Beverly Hills
for a sip and a bite at **Comme Ca** (p58).
If you haven't yet seen a show, look into
the listings and see what's on at the **El
Rey** (p83), **Largo at the Coronet** (p82),
Music Box (p33), **Bootleg Theater**
(p50) or the **Echo** (p53).

Need to Know

For more information, see Survival Guide (p169).

Currency
US dollar ($)

Visas
The US Visa Waiver Program allows visitors from 36 predominantly European countries to travel to the US without a visa. Nationals from all other countries must apply for a tourist visa in advance.

Money
ATMs are widely available and credit cards are accepted in all hotels and most restaurants.

Cell Phones
International cell (mobile) phones will work with roaming. Local SIMs won't sync with European or Asian phones. To save money, get a local Pay As You Go SIM from a Best Buy (www.bestbuy.com) – local phone included for $60. From $15 for SIM only.

Time
Pacific Standard Time (PST; UTC/GMT minus 8 hours) from November to March; Pacific Daylight Savings Time (PDT; UTC/ GMT minus 7 hours) from March to October.

Plugs & Adaptors
LA area outlets demand the North American 20A/120V grounded plug.

Tipping
Tipping is considered mandatory for sit-down, full-service meals. The minimum tip should be 15%. Tip bartenders, too ($1 per drink will suffice).

① Before You Go

Your Daily Budget

Budget less than $100
► Dorm beds from $35
► Excellent supermarkets for self-catering
► Ample free concerts and events

Midrange $200–$250
► Midrange sleeping options from $120
► Two-course dinner and glass of wine $40
► Night out with live music from $50

Top end from $250
► Sleeping options from $250
► Lunch and drinks at industry haunt $75

Useful Websites

Lonely Planet (www.lonelyplanet.com/usa/los-angeles) Destination information, hotel bookings, traveler forum and more.

Los Angeles Downtown News (www.ladowntownnews.com) If it works, eats, drinks, dances or sleeps downtown, this website knows the score.

LA Weekly (www.laweekly.com) LA's trusted indie news and culture rag.

Advance Planning

Three months before Book your hotel and rental car, and secure concert tickets.

One month before Book parking reservations for the Getty; buy tickets for exhibition openings at LACMA or MOCA.

One week before Reserve a table at any top-tier restaurant, and make reservations for high-demand bars and clubs such as La Descarga.

② Arriving in Los Angeles

Los Angeles is more spread out than most major cities, and although there is a downtown, LA is more a quilt with several self-contained neighborhoods knitted together, so the transport details for each neighborhood often vary.

✈ From Los Angeles International Airport (LAX)

Destination	Best Transport
Hollywood, Silver Lake	Metro bus 42, Metro Red Line
Downtown	Metro Red Line, Flyaway Union Station
West Hollywood, Mid-City	Flyaway Westwood, Metro 20/720, Metro 4
Santa Monica	BBB 3
Venice	BBB 3, CC 1
Culver City	Flyaway Westwood, BBB 12
Burbank, Universal City	Flyaway Union Station, Metrolink

③ Getting Around

LA has an automobile pathos. Meaning almost everyone who lives here owns a car, or wishes they did. However, there are multiple public transport options that link up and overlap throughout the LA area.

Ⓜ Metro & Metrolink

The Metro subway system is ever-expanding and links downtown LA with Hollywood, Koreatown, Pasadena, Long Beach, LAX and more. It also connects with Metrolink light-rail service to Burbank and Orange County.

🚌 Bus

The best bus services are offered by LA's Metropolitan Transit Authority (Metro; www.metro.net), which has a handy trip planner on its website, and Santa Monica's Big Blue Bus (BBB; www.bigbluebus.com).

🚗 Taxi

Taxis are quite expensive and should only be used between nearby destinations.

Los Angeles Neighborhoods

West Hollywood & Beverly Hills (p54)

Bling-blessed and sexually ambiguous, stylish, trendy and trashy, here you can eat, shop and drink deeply and without shame.

Burbank & Universal City (p136)

Home to LA's major movie studios, this sprawling grid also has the dubious distinction of being the original world capital of...porn.

◉ Top Sights
Universal Studios

Santa Monica (p88)

Where real-life Lebowskis sip White Russians next to martini-swilling Hollywood producers.

◉ Top Sights
Santa Monica Pier & Beach

◉ *Getty Center*

LACMA ◉

Santa Monica Pier & Beach ◉

Venice (p102)

A boho beach town and longtime haven for artists, New Agers, road-weary tramps, freaks and free spirits.

◉ Top Sights
Venice Boardwalk

Venice Boardwalk ◉

Universal Studios
⊙

Mulholland Drive
⊙

Hollywood Boulevard & the Walk of Fame
⊙

⊙ *Griffith Observatory & Hollywood Sign*

⊙ *La Brea Tar Pits & Page Museum*

⊙ *Walt Disney Concert Hall*

Griffith Park, Silver Lake & Los Feliz (p40)
Old money, boho yuppies and up-and-coming hipsters, it's a neighborhood attuned to far-off galaxies.

⊙ **Top Sights**

Griffith Observatory & Hollywood Sign

Downtown (p118)
Stunning architecture, world-class music, top-notch art, superb dining and sinful cocktails.

⊙ **Top Sights**

Walt Disney Concert Hall

Worth a Trip
⊙ **Top Sights**

Disneyland & Disney California Adventure

Malibu

Getty Center

Mulholland Drive

Miracle Mile & Mid-City (p70)
A blend of history, art and urban culture, Mid-City is sprinkled with museums, top-end shopping and creative kitchens.

⊙ **Top Sights**

La Brea Tar Pits & Page Museum

LACMA

Hollywood (p22)
This is Tinseltown, home of movie studios, flood-lit premieres, the Oscars and so much more.

⊙ **Top Sights**

Hollywood Boulevard & the Walk of Fame

Explore
Los Angeles

Worth a Trip

Downtown LA from the Hollywood Bowl Overlook
WITOLD SKRYPCZAK/LONELY PLANET IMAGES ©

Explore

Hollywood

The neighborhood most synonymous with LA, Hollywood's rise to stardom began with a 1920s ad campaign for Hollywoodland, a residential hillside development with its name announced to the world with towering white letters. Its profound recent renaissance, with restaurants, bars and hotels opening and reopening, even in the midst of a recession, has placed Hollywood back on LA's hotlist.

The Sights in a Day

Grab a Mexican spiced breakfast at the **Loteria Grill** (p29) on **Hollywood Blvd** (p24), then follow the stars with mandatory photo ops at **Grauman's Chinese Theatre** (p25), the **Kodak Theatre** (p25) and **Hollywood Wax Museum** (p29).

Grab lunch at the **Mercantile** (p31) or **Jitlada** (p29), where you can also get a whiff of Hollywood's incredibly authentic Thai Town. Make sure to stop for coconut toffee at **Bhan Kanom Thai** (p37). Now that it's afternoon, you can feel good about a cocktail. If it's a sunny day, enjoy it outdoors at the **Cat & Fiddle** (p31). Otherwise, grab a martini at legendary **Musso & Franks** (p32).

If it's a summer Thursday you can start your evening with sweet views and a glass of vino at **Yamashiro Farmers Market** (p30), otherwise head up to **Oaks Gourmet** (p30) for some wine and one of its famed themed dinners, before catching a superb sketch-comedy show at **Upright Citizens Brigade** (p32). Unless, of course, you have tickets for a show at the **Hollywood Bowl** (p32) – a Hollywood evening that trumps all others.

 Top Sights

Hollywood Boulevard & the Walk of Fame (p24)

Best of Los Angeles

Eating
Sushi Ike (p29)
Jitlada (p29)

Drinking
La Descarga (p31)
Harvard & Stone (p32)

Entertainment
Hollywood Bowl (p32)
Music Box (p33)
Bardot (p34)

Getting There

Ⓜ **Metro** Hollywood is well connected to downtown and Universal City by the Metro Red Line.

Ⓜ **Metro** The most centrally located Red Line stops are Hollywood/Vine and Hollywood/Highland.

🚌 **Bus** MTA, LA's principal transit authority, connects Hollywood with all other parts of town.

Top Sights
Hollywood Boulevard & the Walk of Fame

Hollywood Blvd is one of the most famous of LA's avenues and not least because of the glitterati embedded into the speckled sidewalk. Big Bird, Bob Hope and Marilyn Monroe are among the stars worshipped, photographed and stepped on on the Hollywood Walk of Fame. Since 1960 more than 2400 performers – from legends to long-forgotten players – have been honored with a pink-marble sidewalk star. The galaxy extends from Hollywood Blvd and La Brea Ave to Gower St, and south along Vine St.

◉ Map p26, C3

www.hollywood
chamber.net

Hollywood Blvd btwn La
Brea Ave & Gower St

Ⓜ Hollywood/Highland

Celebrity hand- and footprints outside Grauman's Chinese Theatre

Don't Miss

Grauman's Chinese Theatre

Stand in the footprints of silver-screen legends such as George Clooney in the courtyard of this grand movie palace, built in 1927. **Grauman's Chinese Theatre** (☎323-464-8111; www.chinesetheatres.com; 6925 Hollywood Blvd; courtyard free, adult tickets $10-13; ⌖; MHollywood/Highland) was inspired by Chinese imperial architecture, and the decor extends from the intricate courtyard to the ornate interior.

Kodak Theatre

The Academy Awards are handed out at the **Kodak Theatre** (www.kodaktheatre.com; 6801 Hollywood Blvd; tours adult/child, senior & student $15/10; ☺10:30am-4pm Mon-Fri, 8:30-10:30am Sat & Sun; MHollywood/Highland), which also hosts other big events such as the *American Idol* finals. On the tour you get to sniff around the auditorium, admire a VIP room and see Oscar up close.

Janes House

The **Janes House** (6541 Hollywood Blvd; MHollywood/Highland) is the last remaining Victorian home on Hollywood Blvd. It was built in 1903 and was the former site of Miss Janes' School, which was attended by the children of old Hollywood icons such as Cecil B DeMille, Douglas Fairbanks and Charlie Chaplin. Now? Um, it's a down-market mini-mall.

☑ Top Tips

▶ You can explore the boulevard by day, but it feels so much richer at night, when the stars glitter and the sidewalk stains are (somewhat) hidden.

▶ New stars are born every two or three months, and include a public unveiling by the stars themselves.

▶ There's plenty of kitsch and worse to wade through on what scientists have determined to be among the cheesiest boulevards known to man, but there is also greatness lurking. Exhibit A: Musso & Franks' (p32) martinis.

✗ Take a Break

▶ Loteria Grill (p29) is among the best of the dining options, but Thai Town – a small section of Hollywood Blvd that's packed with tasty, spicy kitchens – is but a short drive away. We love Jitlada (p29) for southern Thai specialties, and Ganda (p31) for Bangkok-style street food.

For reviews see

◉	Top Sights	p24
◉	Sights	p28
✖	Eating	p29
🍷	Drinking	p31
🎭	Entertainment	p32
🔒	Shopping	p36

Runyon Canyon Park

Cahuenga Blvd W

🏠 25

18 🏠

Hollywood Bowl Rd

N Cahuenga Blvd

Hollywood Fwy

Camrose Dr

Hillcrest Rd

4 Hollywood Heritage Museum ◉

Sycamore Ave

Scenic Gardens Ave

Grace Ave

Franklin Ave

Hollywood Franklin Park

Franklin Ave

Franklin Ave

Franklin Ave

Fuller Ave

Cherokee Ave

Whitely Ave

Yucca St

Hollywood/ Highland 🅜 ℹ️

Walk of Fame ◉

🏠 35

✖ 6

N Gardiner St

N Martel Ave

Hawthorn Ave

Hawthorn Ave

Hawthorn Ave

🏠 32

◉ 3

Hollywood Museum

24 🏠

◉

Hollywood Boulevard

30 🏠

Selma Ave

28 🏠

26 🏠

34 🏠 31

9 ✖

N Gardiner St

N Vista St

N Martel Ave

N Fuller Ave

N Poinsettia Pl

N Alta Vista Blvd

N Formosa Ave

N Detroit St

N La Brea Ave

N Orange Dr

N Mansfield Ave

N Highland Ave

29 🏠

13 ✖

🔒 39

W Sunset Blvd

12 ✖

15 🍷

36 🔒 🏠

21

De Longpre Ave

Delongpre Park

Homeland Ave

Fountain Ave

Hollywood Recreation Center

Plummer Park

Lexington Ave

N Ivar Ave

N Cahuenga Blvd

Santa Monica Blvd

Warner Hollywood Studios

Romaine St

N Vista St

Poinsettia Recreation Center

N Poinsettia Pl

N Orange Dr

N Mansfield Ave

N Highland Ave

N Sycamore Ave

N Hudson Ave

Wilcox Ave

Cole Ave

11 ✖

Willoughby Ave

E F G H

1

Griffith
Park

HOLLYWOOD
HILLS

N Beachwood Dr

500 m
0.25 miles

2

Vine St
Argyle Ave
N Gower St
N Bronson Ave

Franklin Ave

Selma Ave
N Van Ness Ave
Taft Ave
N Wilton Pl
Garfield Pl
N Western Ave

Franklin Ave

Russell Ave

Hollywood Fwy

Yucca St

Hollywood Fwy

Carlos Ave

2 Capitol
Records
Tower

23

19 8

5

Hollywood/Vine

20

N Vine St

16 27 CBS
Studios

10

Carlton Way

Carlton Way

37

Hollywood/
Western

N Serrano Ave
N Hobart Blvd
N Kingsley Dr

38 17

Hollywood Blvd

7

N Kingsley Dr

3

W Sunset Blvd

HOLLYWOOD

Afton Pl

22

Lexington Ave

N Gower St
N Beachworth Dr
Gordon St
Tamarind Ave
N Bronson Ave
N Van Ness Ave

La Mirada Ave

Lexington Ave

Virginia Ave

N St Andrews Pl

14

Fountain Ave

4

Virginia Ave

Santa Monica Blvd

Eleanor Ave

N Vine St

1 Hollywood
Forever
Cemetery

Beth Olam
Memorial
Park

N Ridgewood Pl

33

N Oxford Ave

Lemon Grove
Recreation
Center

5

Sights

Hollywood Forever Cemetery
CEMETERY

1 ◉ Map p26, F5

Rock 'n' roll faithful flock to the monument of guitar-playing Johnny Ramone at this Paramount-adjacent boneyard. From Bugsy Siegel's mausoleum, catch the perfectly framed view of the Hollywood sign. Watch outdoor movie screenings in the summer (www.cinespia.org). (☎323-469-1181; www.hollywoodforever.com; 6000 Santa Monica Blvd; admission free, maps $5; 🚌MTA 4)

Capitol Records Tower
LANDMARK

2 ◉ Map p26, E3

You'll quickly recognize this iconic 1956 tower, one of LA's great modern-era buildings. Designed by Welton Becket, it resembles a stack of records topped by a stylus blinking out 'Hollywood' in Morse code. Garth Brooks and John Lennon have their stars outside. (1750 N Vine St; Ⓜ Hollywood/Vine)

Hollywood Museum
MUSEUM

3 ◉ Map p26, C3

Museums on Hollywood Blvd generally fall into the tourist-trap category, but we quite like this slightly musty

Make-up room, Hollywood Museum

DAVID PEEVERS/LONELY PLANET IMAGES ©

and convoluted temple to the stars, housed inside the handsome 1914 art deco Max Factor Building, where the make-up pioneer once worked his magic on Marilyn Monroe and Judy Garland. (☎323-464-7776; www.theholly woodmuseum.com; 1660 N Highland Ave; adult/senior & student/child under 5yr $15/12/5; ⏰10am-5pm Wed-Sun; ☷; Ⓜ Hollywood/Highland)

Hollywood Heritage Museum
MUSEUM

4 Map p26, C2

Hollywood's first feature-length flick, Cecil B DeMille's *The Squaw Man,* was shot in this building between 1913 and 1914. DeMille went on to cofound Paramount. Now the Hollywood Heritage Museum, it's filled with a great collection of costumes, projectors and cameras from the early days of movie-making. (www.hollywoodheritage.org; 2100 N Highland Ave; adult/child under 12yr $7/free; ⏰noon-4pm Wed-Sun; 🚌MTA 156)

Hollywood Wax Museum
MUSEUM

Starved for celeb sightings? Don't fret: at this museum, near the Hollywood Museum (see 3 Map p26; C3), Angelina Jolie, Halle Berry and other red-carpet royalty will stand still – very still – for your camera. This retro haven of kitsch and camp has been around for over 40 years. (www.hollywoodwax. com; 6767 Hollywood Blvd; adult/child/senior $16/9/14; ⏰10am-midnight Sun-Thu, 10am-1am Fri & Sat; ☷; Ⓜ Hollywood/Highland)

Eating

Sushi Ike
JAPANESE $$

5 Map p26, E3

Sweet and tender scallops are sprinkled with sea salt and squeezed with lemon. The broiled octopus is get-outta-here good, and the sashimi comes in thick slabs and always melts in your mouth. Forgive the mini-mall ambience. This fish rocks! (☎323-856-9972; 6051 Hollywood Blvd; mains $8-25; ⏰11:30am-11pm Mon-Fri, noon-11pm Sat; Ⓟ; Ⓜ Hollywood/Vine)

Loteria Grill
MEXICAN $$

6 Map p26, D3

Get your cactus tacos, *mole* burritos and a killer tortilla soup here. It does tasty breakfasts, and the huge L-shaped bar pours over 80 premium tequilas. (www.loteriagrill.com; 6627 Holly-wood Blvd; dishes $3-21; ⏰breakfast, lunch & dinner; Ⓜ Hollywood/Highland)

Jitlada
THAI $$

7 Map p26, H3

A transporting taste of southern Thailand. Its wok-fried catfish and *som tom* (spicy papaya salad) are fantastic, and it counts Matt Groening, Drew Barrymore and Natalie Portman among its loyal, mostly *farang* (non-Thai), customers. (www. jitlada.localthaifood.com; 5233 W Sunset Blvd; ⏰lunch & dinner; Ⓟ; 🚌MTA 2/302)

Oaks Gourmet

DELI $

8 Map p26, F2

A hipster deli and wine shop with a devoted following, its ultimate BLT combines heirloom tomato, creamy Camembert cheese, avocado and black-forest bacon on toasted sourdough, and specialty nights feature grilled sausages (Tuesday), grilled cheese (Wednesday) and tacos (Friday). (📞323-871-8894; www.theoaks gourmet.com; 1915 N Bronson Ave; mains $8.95-11.95; ⏱ breakfast, lunch & dinner; 🅿; 🚌MTA 180, 217)

Q Local Life
The Hollywood Farms

LA's farmers markets supply artisanal kitchens and nourish families across the city. Hollywood has two of the best.

The **Hollywood Farmers Market** (Map p26, E3; www.farmernet.com; Ivar & Selma Ave; ⏱8am-1pm Sun; ♿; Ⓜ Hollywood/Vine) is very much a culinary sprawl with specialty produce from over 90 farmers and over 30 savory prepared-food stalls.

Yamashiro Farmers Market (Map p26, B2; www.yamashirorestaurant .com; 1999 N Sycamore Ave; ⏱5-9pm Thu Apr-Sep; 🅿; 🚌MTA 156) is really more about the views from Yamashiro's spectacular perch. Gourmet food stalls serve up delights such as miso cod tacos, grilled bratwurst and Bulgarian gelato. There's a wine-tasting bar, and live music too.

Both markets are definitely great events for the whole family.

Cheebo

CALIFORNIAN $$

9 Map p26, A3

This funky, all-natural California-chic cafe makes heaping salads, bulging sandwiches and organic pizzas. Kids love the free paper and crayons and special menu in the afternoons. (📞323-850-7070; www.cheebo.com; 7533 W Sunset Blvd; mains $10-26; ⏱8am-midnight; 🍴♿; 🚌MTA 2)

Roscoe's House of Chicken & Waffles

AMERICAN $

10 Map p26, E3

It's not spiffy, the lighting's not so great, and the decor's best described as well worn and wooden. But for LA's best Southern soul food, look no further than this 30-year-old landmark where the combo may sound strange, but the namesake dish is can't-miss. (📞323-466-7453; www.roscoeschickenand waffles.com; 1514 N Gower St; mains $8-16; ⏱8am-midnight Mon-Thu & Sun, 8:30am-4am Fri, 8am-4am Sat; ♿; Ⓜ Hollywood/Vine)

Providence

AMERICAN FUSION $$$

11 Map p26, D5

This sublime dining room with two Michelin stars has long been one of LA's finest. To truly sample Michael Cimarusti's talents, splurge for the nine-course tasting menu. (📞323-460-

4170; www.providencela.com; 5955 Melrose Ave; mains from $25; ☺lunch Fri, dinner daily; P; ▢MTA 10)

Mercantile
MARKET CAFE $$

12 Map p26, D4

A fun, brick-walled, concrete-floored loft outfitted with a cheese case, a wine bar, shelves of gourmet oils, mustards, jams and more. It also whips up smoked-trout crostinis, foie gras terrines, Cuban sandwiches and plate lunches. (www.themercantilela.com; 6600 Sunset Blvd; dishes $5-16; ☺lunch & dinner; P; ▢MTA)

Life Food Organic
ORGANIC $

13 Map p26, D3

With recipes gleaned from the wild-souled, raw-powered madman, Dr David Jubbs, it serves the healthiest fast food around. Have a chocolate shake made with almond milk, a veggie chili burger with a sesame seaweed salad on the side, and a chocolate cream pie for dessert. (www.lifefoodorganic.com; 1507 N Cahuenga Ave; juices & mains from $6; ☺breakfast, lunch & dinner; Ⓜ Hollywood/Vine)

Ganda
THAI $

Sample authentic Bangkok night-market cuisine at this pick-and-mix steam table of stewed, fried and broiled seafood, chicken and veggie dishes. Ganda, next to Bhan Kanom Thai (see 38 🔒 Map p26; H3), stays open until 2am during the week and 3am on weekends. (5269 Hollywood Blvd; dishes $6-14; ☺lunch & dinner; P; ⓂHollywood/Western)

Drinking

La Descarga
LOUNGE

14 Map p26, G4

This tastefully frayed, sublimely sweaty rum and cigar lounge is a revelation. Behind the marble bar are over 100 rum varieties from Haiti and Guayana, Guatemala and Venezuela. It mixes and muddles specialty cocktails, but you'd do well to order something aged, and sip it neat as you enjoy the burlesque ballerina on the catwalk. Reservations are mandatory. (☏323-466-1324; www.ladescargala.com; 1159 N Western Ave; ☺8pm-2am Tue-Sat; ▢MTA 4, 207)

Cat & Fiddle
PUB

15 Map p26, D4

From Morrissey to Frodo, you never know who might be sipping Guinness on the leafy, laid-back courtyard patio where it's more about friends and conversation than faux-hawks and working the deal. (☏323-468-3800; www.thecatandfiddle.com; 6530 Sunset Blvd; ☺11:30am-2am; ▢MTA 2)

The Well
LOUNGE

16 Map p26, E3

Always a consistent winner due to its tasty cocktails, rock 'n' roll soundtrack, dark interior, plush booths and sexy staff (of both genders). Bartenders and servers from across town often spend their downtime here. (www.myspace/thewellhollywood; 1536 Argyle Ave; ⏰5pm-2am; 🅿; 🚇MTA 2)

Harvard & Stone BAR

17 Map p26, H3

A whiskey bar with an industrial minitheme (steel front door, antiquated mining tools, wrought-iron furnishings). Owned by the brothers

> ### ⃝ Local Life
> ### Legendary Lairs
>
> Hollywood history hangs thick in the air at **Musso & Franks Grill** (Map p26, C3; 📞323-467-7788; 6667 Hollywood Blvd; ⏰11am-11pm Tue-Sat; 🚇Hollywood/Highland).
>
> Charlie Chaplin used to slam gimlets at the bar and Raymond Chandler penned scripts in the high-backed booths. Mick Jagger and Woody Allen are also fans of the noir ambience, gentlemen bartenders and icy martinis served in small stems.
>
> A recent classic, the **Writer's Room** (Map p26, C3; 6685 Hollywood Blvd; ⏰9pm-2am Thu-Sat; 🚇Hollywood/Highland) used to be the backroom at Musso & Franks when Fitzgerald and Hemmingway mingled with starlets. It was recently reopened by NYC nightlife impresarios, backed by actor Jason Segal and other Hollywood heads. Expect craftsman booze, soaring ceilings and a fine brick bar.

who opened La Descarga, the thing here is craftsman whiskey, bourbon and cocktail specials that rotate daily. It lures hipsters with live bands, burlesque troops and solid DJs. (www.harvardandstone.com; 5221 Hollywood Blvd; ⏰8pm-2am; 🚇Hollywood/Western)

Entertainment

Hollywood Bowl CONCERT VENUE

18 Map p26, C1

Summers in LA just wouldn't be the same without this chill spot for symphonies under the stars, and big-name acts from Baaba Maal to Sigur Rós to Radiohead to Paul McCartney. The nation's largest natural amphitheater, the Hollywood Bowl has been around since 1922. Pack a boozy picnic. Alcohol is permitted. (📞323-850-2000; www.hollywoodbowl.com; 2301 N Highland Ave; admission from $1; ⏰late Jun-late Sep; 👶; 🚇Hollywood/Highland)

Upright Citizens Brigade COMEDY

19 Map p26, F2

Founded in New York by *Saturday Night Live* alums Amy Poehler and Ian Roberts along with Matt Besser and Matt Walsh, this sketch-comedy group cloned itself in Hollywood in 2005 and is arguably the best improv theater in town. Most shows are $5 or $8 but Sunday's 'Asssscat' is freeeee. (www.ucbtheatre.com; 5919 Franklin Ave; admission $5-8; 🚌MTA 180, 217)

ArcLight & Cinerama Dome

Music Box
LIVE MUSIC

20 ⭐ Map p26, E3

The old Henry Fonda theater remains one of Hollywood's best venues for live music. It's an intimate, general-admission space with an open dance floor and balcony seating. It books the best progressive rock bands (think Mumford & Sons and Broken Bells) around. (www.themusicbox.la; 6126 Hollywood Blvd; admission varies; P; MHollywood/Vine)

ArcLight & Cinerama Dome
CINEMA

21 ⭐ Map p26, D4

Assigned seats and exceptional celeb-sighting potential make this 14-screen multiplex the best around. If your taste dovetails with its schedule, the awesome 1963 geodesic Cinerama Dome is a must. Parking is $3 for four hours. (📞323-464-4226; www.arclight cinemas.com; 6360 W Sunset Blvd; adult $12-14.50, child 3-12yr $9-10; 👶; 🚌MTA 2)

El Floridita
LATIN

22 ⭐ Map p26, E4

The place for grown-up *salseros*. Order a mojito and watch the beautiful dancers do their thing. The Monday-night jams led by Johnny Polanco y su Orquesta Amistad are legendary; make reservations at least a week in advance. (📞323-871-8612; www.elfloridita. com; 1253 N Vine St; cover $10, free with dinner; ⏰Mon, Wed, Fri & Sat; 🚌MTA 210)

Bardot
CLUB

23 ⭐ Map p26, E3

Two bars, two floors, blood-red walls, ornate concrete moldings and more dog paintings than seems reasonable are tucked behind and above Club Avalon. Monday nights mean **School Night** (www.itsaschoolnight.com), hosted by KCRW's Chris Douridas – a live music club featuring buzz-worthy talent. (www.bardothollywood.com; 1737 N Vine St; ⏰varies Mon-Sat; **P**; **M**Hollywood/Vine)

American Cinematheque & Egyptian Theatre
CINEMA

24 ⭐ Map p26, C3

If nonprofits make you yawn, we promise this one won't. Its tributes, retrospectives and foreign films are presented in the King Tut's–tomb-inspired Egyptian Theatre. Directors, screenwriters and actors often swing by for postshow Q&As. (☎323-466-3456; www.americancinematheque.com; 6712 Hollywood Blvd; adult/senior & student $11/9; ⏰Wed-Sun; **M**Hollywood/Highland; ♿)

Ford Amphitheatre
CONCERT VENUE

25 ⭐ Map p26, D1

Every seat is within 100ft of the stage at this up-close-and-personal outdoor amphitheater. With the Hollywood Hills as a backdrop, catch indie bands, foreign movies and dance troupes from June to October. Picnics welcome. (☎323-461-3673; www.fordamphitheatre.com; 2580 Cahuenga Blvd E; admission $5-45; ♿; 🚌MTA 156, 222)

Hotel Café
LIVE MUSIC

26 ⭐ Map p26, D3

Unsigned bands get their due at the charmingly intimate Hotel Café. Seen as a stepping-stone for up-and-comers, the calendar has included an eclectic mix – from touring Australian cult faves John Butler Trio to rock legends such as Pete Townsend. (☎323-461-2040; www.hotelcafe.com; 1623 N Cahuenga Blvd; admission $10-12; ⏰shows nightly; **M**Hollywood/Vine)

Hollywood Palladium
CONCERT VENUE

27 ⭐ Map p26, E3

This art deco classic, built in 1940 and christened by the Chairman of the Board (Sinatra), has long been a favorite for its open-floor, general-admission intimacy. It's hosted everyone from Hendrix to James Brown to Madonna to Jay-Z. (www.livenation.com; 6215 W Sunset Blvd; admission varies; **P**; 🚌MTA 2)

IO West
COMEDY

28 ⭐ Map p26, D3

Toss out the phrase 'giant mushroom' and watch the cast spin a 45-minute skit. Long form is the specialty at the LA branch of Olympic Improv Chicago, where you might catch familiar faces from *The Office* or *Saturday Night Live* honing their comedy chops. (☎323-962-7560; www.iowest.com; 6366 Hollywood Blvd; admission $5-10; **M**Hollywood/Vine)

Avalon

CLUB

Big name DJs appear for Avalon's Saturday-night electronic dance party 'Avaland,' but this 18-and-over, 1400-capacity club next to Bardot (see 23 Map p26; E3) rocks on Thursday and Friday nights, too. With its late-night permit, you'll see Avalon party kids spilling out onto the sidewalk around the same time that the sun comes up. (☎323-462-8900; www.avalon hollywood.com; 1735 N Vine St; admission $20; ⓂHollywood/Vine)

Catalina Bar & Grill

JAZZ

29 Map p26, C3

The exterior of LA's smoothest jazz club looks more like an office complex than a sexy club, but once inside the spacious and sultry digs, all is forgiven. Dizzy Gillespie, Art Blakely and the Marsalis brothers have graced the stage, but up-and-comers are spotlighted too. (☎323-466-2210; www.catalinajazzclub.com; 6725 W Sunset Blvd; ⓂHollywood/Highland)

Sayer's Club

CLUB

30 Map p26, D3

An ultra-exclusive, A-list lounge accessed through a quasi-speakeasy entrance off the Papaya King. You'll most likely need to drop your industry contacts just to get in, but if you do manage it, you'll enjoy secret live music acts, $18 cocktails and lots of well-known faces. (www.sbe.com/thesayersclub; 1645 Wilcox Ave; Ⓟ; ⓂHollywood/Highland)

Roxbury

CLUB

31 Map p26, D3

With massive dance parties attuned to touring turntable ninjas, this new hot spot (no, it isn't the Roxbury of Will Ferrell/Chris Kattan fame) attracts the pretty people, and protects the gate with a rope and a list, so make arrangements in advance. (☎323-469-0040; www.roxbury.la; 1661 Ivar Ave; Ⓟ; ⓂHollywood/Vine)

El Capitan Theatre

CINEMA

32 Map p26, C3

Disney rolls out family-friendly blockbusters at this movie palace, often with costumed characters putting on the Ritz in live preshow routines. The best seats are on the balcony in the middle of the front row. VIP tickets ($20) allow you to reserve a seat and include popcorn and a beverage. (www.elcapitan.go.com; 6838 Hollywood Blvd; adult/child & senior from $12/9; ♿; ⓂHollywood/Highland)

MET Theatre

THEATER

33 Map p26, G5

Holly Hunter and Ed Harris have strutted on the MET's stage, and Dustin Hoffman and Angelina Jolie have funneled in some cash. The fare here runs from edgy to traditional and has included the premiere of Sam Shepard's *Curse of the Starving Class*. (www.themettheatre.com; 1089 N Oxford Ave; tickets from $15; Ⓟ; 🚌MTA 4, 207)

Club Ecco
CLUB

34  Map p26, D3

This cozy club merits mention because it used sustainably forested timber, paperless drywall and nontoxic paint during construction, and utilizes LED lighting and green power. Of course, none of that truly matters if the club isn't any fun. It tackles that problem by rotating local and international DJs of note, who keep the party bumping. (www.eccohollywood.com; 1640 N Cahuenga Ave; **P**; **M** Hollywood/Vine)

Colony
CLUB

35 Map p26, D3

Just over a year old, still hot, and drawing celebs and scenesters on the regular, it's going for a Hamptons in Hollywood angle. The indoor–outdoor flow, shutters and boardwalk do feel beachy, and the clientele is mostly young and, of course, usually beautiful. (323-525-2450; www.sbe.com/thecolony; 1743 N Cahuenga Blvd; **P**; **M** Hollywood/Vine)

Shopping

Amoeba Music
MUSIC

36 Map p26, D4

Click, click, click…is the sound of scores of customers you'll see flipping through some half-a-million new and used CDs, DVDs, videos and vinyl at this granddaddy of all music stores.

Posters at Amoeba Music

There are handy listening stations, and its outstanding *Music We Like* booklet keeps you from buying lemons. Check the website for free in-store live performances by touring bands. (📞323-245-6400; www.amoeba.com; 6400 Sunset Blvd; 🕐10:30am-11pm Mon-Sat, 11am-9pm Sun; 🅿; 🚇MTA 2)

Mush
GIFTS, HOMEWARES

37 Map p26, G3

An inspiring gift, antique and home-decor boutique that is filled with color (we very much dig those resin lanterns), style (you'll love the silver jewelry and mod furniture) and soul (stone Buddha, anyone?). The music and the owner-operator are warm and groovy. (www.m-u-s-h.com; 5651 Hollywood Blvd; 🚇Hollywood/Western)

Bhan Kanom Thai
FOOD & DRINK

38 🔒 Map p26, H3

Next door to Ganda is a remarkable sweet shop. It has all manner of Thai desserts, including candy (the coconut toffee is a must), dried fruit, gum-mies, sours, crisps and cakes. (www.bhankanomthai.com; 5271 Hollywood Blvd; 🕐10am-2am; 🅿; 🚇Hollywood/Western)

Counterpoint
MUSIC, BOOKS

At Counterpoint, located near the Upright Citizens Brigade (see 19 ⭐ Map p26, F2), woodblock stacks are packed high with used fiction, while crude plywood bins are likewise stuffed with vinyl soul, classical and jazz. The real gems are in the collectible wing next door. (www.counterpointrecordsandbooks.com; 5911 Franklin Ave; 🕐11am-11pm Tue-Sat, 1-9:30pm Sun, 11am-9:30pm Mon; 🚇MTA 180, 217)

Space 15 Twenty
MALL

39 Map p26, D3

The hippest mini-mall in Hollywood, this designer construct of brick, wood, concrete and glass is home to classic and trendsetting SoCal minichains such as Umami Burger, Hennesy & Ingalls and Free People. (www.space1520.com; 1520 N Cahuenga Blvd; 🕐11am-9pm Mon-Fri, 10am-10pm Sat, to 9pm Sun; 🅿; 🚇Hollywood/Vine)

Top Sights
Mulholland Drive

Getting There

🚗 **Car** You can access Mulholland via the I-405 (exit Mulholland Dr) or from Highland, Cahuenga or Laurel Canyon in Hollywood, Coldwater Canyon in Beverly Hills or Beverly Glen in Bel Air.

This legendary road winds and dips for 24 miles through the Santa Monica Mountains, delivering iconic views of downtown, Hollywood and the San Fernando Valley at each bend. On clear winter days, the panorama opens up from the snowcapped San Gabriel Mountains to the shimmering Pacific Ocean.

Don't Miss

Runyon Canyon

A chaparral cut in the Hollywood Hills, **Runyon Canyon** (www.lamountains.com; 2000 N Fuller Ave; ☉dawn-dusk) is a 130-acre public park as famous for its beautiful, bronzed and buff runners as it is for the panoramic views from the upper ridge. You can park in the pull-out off of Mulholland Dr, then follow the trail to a wider, partially paved fire road that winds down the canyon past the remains of the Runyon estate.

Coldwater Canyon Park

Home to the tremendous local nonprofit TreePeople, which has been restoring LA's watershed for 30-plus years, this lovely **park** (www.laparks.org; 12601 N Mulholland Dr; ☉dawn-dusk; P) has trail access all the way down to the valley floor.

Stargazing

If you're lucky enough to have a convertible, then you can stargaze the traditional way, as there are no streetlights on Mulholland at night. Or you can stalk famous people as you skirt the mansions of the rich and famous. According to sources, Jack Nicholson's city house is at No 12850, Warren and Annette at No 13671. Pick up a current *Star Map* and you'll find others.

☑ Top Tips

▶ Driving the entire route, from the dirt road in Brentwood to Highland in Hollywood, takes about an hour.

▶ If you don't have much time, drive up to the Hollywood Bowl Overlook for classic views of the Hollywood sign.

▶ Don't be afraid to turn down canyon roads such as Outpost, or Laurel Tce.

✗ Take a Break

Laurel Canyon, that artsy bohemian enclave that nurtured Hal Ashby in the '70s, and inspired Frances McDormand's star turn as a free-thinking music producer in the film of the same name, is worth a stop. There's a local grocer, and **Pace** (☎310-654-8583; www.peaceinthe canyon.com; 2100 Laurel Canyon Blvd; ☉dinner; P♿), frequented by local celebs.

Explore

Griffith Park, Silver Lake & Los Feliz

Los Feliz, founded by mining mogul Griffith J Griffith, is one of LA's oldest, most affluent neighborhoods. Swingers spot-lit its hipster haunts (and traits) in the mid-90s, when high rents chased up-and-comers to Silver Lake's revitalized modernist homes, boho bistros and bars. But for all the history and palpable urban cool, the highlight here remains the 4210-acre Griffith Park.

The Sights in a Day

☀ Take your breakfast at the **Alcove** (p47), alongside hipsters, yuppies and the occasional star (we saw Jason Schwartzman and Zooey Deschanel dine together here), then spend the rest of the morning breezing through boutiques and thrift shops on Hillhurst and Vermont. Don't miss **Spitfire Girl** (p50), **Co-Op 28** (p50) or **Skylight Books** (p50), then check out Frank Lloyd Wright's masterful **Hollyhock House** (p46).

☼ Grab lunch at **Forage** (p48) in Silver Lake, before exploring the bohemian boutiques that define Silver Lake, such as **Matrushka Construction** (p50) and **Driftwood** (p51). Then double back to **Griffith Park** (pictured left; p47) and spend the late afternoon and early evening exploring the **Griffith Observatory** (p42) and enjoying some of the city's most magnificent views.

☾ If it's a clear, dark night, linger along the lawns around the Observatory and peer into telescopes toward heavenly bodies. Then join the crowds gabbing and grubbing on the **Café Stella** (p47) patio for a Parisian supper, before hitting **4100 Bar** (p49) or **Thirsty Crow** (p49) for drinks into the night. Or if your timing is impeccable, ditch the cocktails and see a show at the **Greek Theatre** (p50).

◉ Top Sights
Griffith Observatory & Hollywood Sign (p42)

♥ Best of Los Angeles

Eating
Forage (p48)

Yuca's (p48)

Flore (p48)

Imbibing
Good (p49)

Buying
Spitfire Girl (p50)

Wacko (p51)

Getting There

Ⓜ **Metro** The area is well connected to Hollywood, Downtown and Universal City by the Metro Red Line.

Ⓜ **Metro** The most centrally located Red Line stop is Vermont/Sunset.

🚌 **Bus** MTA, LA's principal transit authority, connects Los Feliz and Silver Lake with all other parts of town. The LADOT Observatory Shuttle operates on weekends.

Top Sights
Griffith Observatory & Hollywood Sign

Two world-famous landmarks loom from either end of Griffith Park in the Hollywood Hills. The 1935 Griffith Observatory opens a window onto the universe from its perch on the southern slopes of Mt Hollywood. LA's most famous landmark is just west of the park, and first appeared in 1923 as an advertising gimmick for a real-estate development called 'Hollywoodland.' The last four letters were lopped off in the '40s. Alice Cooper and Hugh Hefner joined forces with fans to save the famous symbol in the 1970s.

◉ Map p44, A2 & B4

2800 E Observatory Rd, Griffith Park; Hollyridge Trailhead, Beachwood Dr

admission free

⊘ observatory noon-10pm Wed-Fri, from 10am Sat & Sun

Griffith Observatory and view across LA

Don't Miss

Samuel Oschin Planetarium

Featuring a renovated interior, state-of-the-art star projector and laser projection systems, and one of the largest planetarium domes in the world, the observatory's planetarium shows (adult/child under 12 $7/5) are one of the biggest draws. Shows bounce from the origins of the universe and our place within it, to the search for water in the solar system to an exploration of Viking cosmology featuring a Northern Lights display that will blow your mind.

Rooftop Vistas

Head to the roof to peek through the refracting and solar telescopes housed in the smaller domes. The sweeping views of the Hollywood Hills and the gleaming city below are just as spectacular, especially at sunset.

Hollyridge Trail

Okay, so you desperately, compulsively, must hike to the Hollywood Sign where in 1932 a struggling young actress named Peggy Entwistle leapt her way into local lore (and her own death) from the letter 'H'. Take Beachwood Dr from Franklin until its end at the Hollyridge Trailhead. Follow the trail (don't worry, there are signs), make a left at the first fork and a right at the second fork. Expect spectacular views along the way. You'll wind up behind the letters, which are fenced off to preserve them from would-be vandals. Bring plenty of water. The hike takes about an hour.

☑ Top Tips

▶ It helps to have a car to explore Griffith Park, but you can access the observatory via public transport on weekends (10am to 10pm). Take the Metro to Vermont/Sunset and hop the LADOT shuttle (25¢, 35 minutes) from there.

▶ Stay after dark to peer into the Zeist Telescope on the eastside of the roof; staff wheel additional telescopes out to the front lawn if you can't be bothered to wait in line for the Zeist.

▶ If you'd rather not hike up to the fenced-off letters themselves, good viewing spots include from Hollywood & Highland, the top of Beachwood Dr and the Griffith Observatory.

✕ Take a Break

Both the Hollyridge Trail and Griffith Observatory lawn demand a picnic, and there's no better place to stock up than the Oaks Gourmet (p30), a five-minute drive away.

1 km
0.5 miles

N

W Colorado Blvd

W Broadway

Los Feliz Blvd

Glendale Water
Reclamation
Plant

North
Atwater
Park

Los Angeles River

Golden State Fwy

Los Feliz Blvd

Museum
of the
American West

3

Wilson Golf
Course

Crystal Springs Dr

LA Zoo &
Botanical Gardens 2

Los
Angeles Zoo

Harding
Golf
Course

Vista del Valle Dr

Commonwealth
Ave

Roosevelt
Municipal Golf
Course

N Vermont Ave

Griffith Park

Mt Bell ▲

▲ Mt Hollywood

Mt Hollywood Dr

Vermont Canyon Rd

14 ✪

Griffith Park Dr

Mulholland Hwy

Mt Chapel ▲

Brush
Canyon

Western Canyon Dr

Griffith
Observatory ◉

Forest Lawn
Memorial Park
& Hollywood Hills

Sennet
Canyon

Mt Lee Dr
▲ Mt Lee

◉ Hollywood
Sign

Hollyridge Trail

Canyon Dr

A

B

C

D

E

1

2

3

4

Riverside Dr

Rowena Reservoir

Silver Lake Reservoir

Reservoir St

N Benton Way

Marathon St

Micheltorena St

SILVER LAKE

W Sunset Blvd

Silver Lake Blvd

Griffith Park Blvd

Hyperion Ave

✕ 4

Micheltorena St

🚇 11

Silver Lake Blvd

Marathon St

St George St

Effie St

Edgecliff Dr

Bellevue Recreation Center

15 ✪

Sunset Dr

✕ 8

🍴 13

Lucile Ave

Sanborn Ave

Hyperion Ave

Marathon St

Myra Ave

5 ✕

10

N Hoover St

N Hoover St

N Hoover St

Hollywood Fwy

Clayton Ave

6 ✕

12

N Virgil Ave

7 ✕✕

9

Hillhurst Ave

Russell Ave

Melbourne Ave

Kingswell Ave

Prospect Ave

Burns Ave

Monroe St

17 🏠

🏠 18

Vermont Ave

16 🏠

N 🏠 19

Finley Ave

Franklin Ave

LOS FELIZ

Barnsdall Art Park

1 ✪

Hollywood Blvd

Hollyhock House

Ⓜ Vermont/ Sunset

Lexington Ave

Vermont/Santa Monica/LACC Ⓜ

Los Angeles City College

Monroe St

Hollywood Fwy

Beverly Blvd

C

Los Feliz Blvd

Hollywood/ Western Ⓜ

W Sunset Blvd

Fountain Ave

Santa Monica Blvd

Romaine Ave

N Western Ave

Melrose Ave

B

Franklin Ave

Hollywood Blvd

N Western Ave

Hollywood Fwy

N Bronson Ave

Hollywood Forever Cemetery

Beth Olam Memorial Park

A

For reviews see	
◆ Top Sights	p42
◉ Sights	p46
✕ Eating	p47
🍴 Drinking	p49
✿ Entertainment	p50
🛍 Shopping	p50

5

6

7

8

Sights

Hollyhock House
LANDMARK

1 🎯 Map p44, C6

Oil heiress Aline Barnsdall commissioned Frank Lloyd Wright to design this hilltop home in 1919. As happens with rich eccentrics and stubborn geniuses, the project ended sourly and was finished by architect Rudolph Schindler. Due to Wright's Romanza-style design there's an easy flow between rooms and courtyards. Note abstract imagery of the hollyhock, Aline's preferred flower, throughout. (☎323-644-6269; www.hollyhockhouse. net; Barnsdall Art Park, 4800 Hollywood Blvd, Los Feliz; adult/senior & 12-17yr/under 12yr $7/3/2, cash only; ⊙tours hourly 12:30-3:30pm Fri-Sun; P; MVermont/Sunset)

LA Zoo & Botanical Gardens
ZOO

2 🎯 Map p44, D1

The Los Angeles Zoo with its 1100 finned, feathered and furry friends from more than 250 species rarely fails to enthrall the little ones. What began in 1912 as a refuge for retired circus animals now brings in more than a million visitors each year. (☎323-644-4200; www.lazoo.org; 5333 Zoo Dr, Griffith Park; adult/senior/2-12yr $14/11/9; ⊙10am-5pm; ⌷; ⎕MTA 96)

Museum of the American West

Museum of the American West

MUSEUM

3 ⊙ Map p44, D1

Unabashed exhibits on the good, the bad and the violent during America's westward expansion rope in even the most reluctant of cowpokes. Here are Annie Oakley's shotgun, a Concord stagecoach ('It don't break down, it only wears out') and one of Gene Autry's fabled guitars. (☏323-667-2000; www.autrynationalcenter.org; 4700 Western Heritage Way, Griffith Park; adult/senior & student/3-12yr/under 3yr $10/6/4/free; ⊙10am-4pm Tue-Fri, 11am-5pm Sat & Sun, to 8pm Thu Jul & Aug; P♿; 🚆MTA 96)

Eating

Barbrix

TAPAS $$

4 ✗ Map p44, E6

As stylish and laidback as Silver Lake, this wine and tapas bar with its horseshoe wine bar, exposed beams and open kitchen has plenty of room inside and out. Go cold with *hamachi* (yellowtail) crudo and charcuterie, or heat up with veal meatballs, seared scallops and blistered *shishito* peppers. (☏323-662-2442; www.barbrix.com; 2442 Hyperion Ave; plates $6-17; ⊙dinner; P; 🚆MTA 175)

Café Stella

FRENCH $$$

5 ✗ Map p44, D7

As charming as it gets, Café Stella is a cloud of clinking glasses, red wine,

Local Life
Griffith Park

A gift to the city in 1896 by mining mogul Griffith J Griffith, **Griffith Park** (Map p44, C2; ☏323-913-4688; www.lacity.org/rap; 4730 Crystal Springs Dr; admission free; ⊙park 6am-10pm, hiking paths, bridle trails & mountain roads to sunset; P♿; 🚆MTA 180, 181) is LA's playground with facilities for all age levels and interests. At five times the size of New York's Central Park, it is one of the country's largest urban green spaces and its 53 miles of hiking trails are the domain of local families whenever the sun shines. Stop by the ranger's office for a map and list of attractions.

good jazz and classic French bistro cuisine under a tented patio and rambling into an antiquated dining room. Artful and reasonable, it bustles at lunch and is packed for dinner. There's a reason. (☏323-666-0265; www.cafestella.com; 3932 W Sunset Blvd; mains $18-35; ⊙lunch & dinner; P; 🚆MTA 2)

Alcove

CAFE $$

6 ✗ Map p44, C5

Hillhurst's choice breakfast hang, this sunny cafe spills onto a multilevel streetside brick patio. It's housed in a restored 1897 Spanish-style duplex, and the food is ridiculously good. There's crab cake Benedict, bison chili omelettes, and crepes stuffed with espresso-infused cream. If you loathe standing in line, belly up to the marble Big Bar, order from the barkeep and pair your meal with a craftsman, cracked-ice cocktail. (www.alcovecafe.com; 1929 Hillhurst Ave; mains $12-15; ⏰breakfast, lunch & dinner; **P** **🚻**; 🚇MTA 180, 181)

Little Dom's
ITALIAN $$

 7 🍴 Map p44, C5

An understated, yet stylish, Italian deli and restaurant with deep booths, marble tables and wood floors. It has dynamite kale salad, antipasti and sandwiches – especially the fried-oyster po'boy. Pop into the deli for takeout.(📞323-661-0055; 2128

Interior, Hollyhock House (p46)

Hillhurst Ave; mains $10-15; ⏰8am-3pm & from 6pm; 🚇MTA 180, 181)

Forage
MARKET, CAFE $$

 8 🍴 Map p44, D7

Ignore the somewhat soulless design and pair a protein (*jidori* chicken or flank steak) with a couple of gourmet deli salads. Or just nibble on a quiche or crostini. It's all delicious here. Hence the packed house. (www.foragela.com; 3823 W Sunset Ave; mains $7-13; ⏰lunch & dinner Tue-Sat; 🚇MTA 2)

Yuca's
MEXICAN $

9 🍴 Map p44, C5

Location, location, location…is definitely not what lures people to this parking-lot snack shack. It's the tacos, stupid! And the *tortas,* burritos and other Mexi faves that earned the Herrera family the coveted James Beard Award in 2005. (📞323-662-1214; 2056 Hillhurst Ave; mains $2-4; ⏰11am-6pm Mon-Sat; 🚻; 🚇MTA 180, 181)

Flore
VEGAN $$

 10 Map p44, D7

If you're more hippie than hipster, you'll want to sink into a reclaimed diner booth and feast on tofu scrambles, raw *jicima* (yam bean) or cooked seitan tacos served in stone-ground-corn tortillas. Don't sleep on those cupcakes. (www.florevegan.com; 3818 W Sunset Blvd; mains $9-11; ⏰lunch Mon, lunch & dinner Tue-Sun; **P**; 🚇MTA 2)

Skylight Books (p50)

Drinking

Thirsty Crow   BAR

11 ⬤ Map p44, D8

A loving ode to the fiery sweetness
that is a classic small-batch Kentucky
bourbon (it has more than 60 kinds).
Yes, the bartenders can mix and muddle
fresh craftsman cocktails. But, puleeeze,
do Uncle Jessup proud, and sip yours
neat. It has live music every Sunday.
(www.thirstycrowbar.com; 2939 W Sunset Blvd;
⊙5pm-2am Mon-Sat, 2pm-2am Sun; ⬛MTA 2)

4100 Bar   BAR

12 ⬤ Map p44, D7

Past the bouncer and the thick velvet
curtain awaits this good-looking bar
with an unpretentious and omni-
sexual crowd, a jukebox heavy on
alt-rock, and bartenders who've been
around the block...twice. (www.4100bar.
com; 4100 W Sunset Blvd; ⊙7pm-2am; ℗;
⬛MTA 2)

Good   MICROBREW

13 ⬤ Map p44, D7

Think: 500 microbrews from
California, Belgium, Brazil, the Czech
Republic. It serves flights, tableside
draft towers, and on Wednesday it's
'mystery beer' night. The bartender
will pour the beer of his choosing for
just $3. (www.goodmicrobrew.com; 3920
W Sunset Blvd; ⊙11am-10pm Mon-Thu, to
11pm Fri, 9am-11pm Sat, to 10pm Sun; ℗;
⬛MTA 2)

Entertainment

Greek Theatre
PERFORMING ARTS

14 ⭐ Map p44, C4

Appreciative summer crowds love the vibe and the variety – Erykah Badu to Willie Nelson – at this 5800-seat outdoor venue tucked in the woodsy hills of Griffith Park. Be forewarned, parking is stacked, so plan on a post-show wait. (☎323-665-5857; www.greektheatrela.com; 2700 N Vermont Ave, Griffith Park; ☺early May-early Nov; 🚍MTA 180, 181)

Bootleg Theater
THEATER

15 ⭐ Map p44, D8

Part progressive-rock and folk venue, part theater space, part multidisciplinary arts foundation and laboratory. This restored 1930s warehouse hosts one-off shows and long-term residencies for edgy indie bands. It also supports spoken word, dance and dramatic artists pushing boundaries and creating beautiful works. (www.bootlegtheater.org; 2220 Beverly Blvd; 🅿; 🚍MTA 14, 37)

Shopping

Skylight Books
BOOKS

16 🔒 Map p44, C5

Like moths to the skylight, folks are drawn to this brick-house loftlike indie bookstore focusing on local, nontraditional and foreign authors. It also hosts several book groups and runs meet-the-author events.

(☎323-660-1175; www.skylightbooks.com; 1818 N Vermont Ave, Los Feliz; ☺10am-10pm; Ⓜ Vermont/Sunset)

Matrushka Construction
FASHION

Who says fashion has to be superficial? Lara Howe crafts her sublime tailored designs from remnant fabrics personally and locally sourced by the owner-operator. The fabrics at Matrushka, near Flore (see 10 Map p44, D7), are still top notch; they are simply either vintage or discarded by large corporate manufacturers. (www.matrushka.com; 3822 W Sunset Blvd; 🚍MTA 2)

Spitfire Girl
GIFTS

17 🔒 Map p44, C5

The new Los Feliz location of the Echo Park original offers a slightly more refined take on quirk. It trades in, well, almost anything, but especially gift and photography books, its own stuffed-gnome and throw-pillow line (that's how the business launched), and organic and aromatic candles and soaps. (www.spitfiregirl.com; 1939 Hillhurst Ave; 🚍MTA 180, 181)

Co-Op 28
GIFTS, GALLERY

18 🔒 Map p44, C6

A fabulous new boutique and gallery space offering only handmade or indie goods. The art gallery in the back is alive with energy, and please pay your respects to Pretzel, the most charming dalmatian in LA. (www.facebook.com/coop28handmade; 1728 N Vermont Ave;

Wacko

⌚11am-7pm Mon-Wed, Sat, to 9pm Thu-Fri, noon-6pm Sun; **M**Vermont/Sunset)

Wacko COLLECTIBLES

19 🔒 Map p44, C6

Billy Shire's giftorium of camp and kitsch has been a fun browse for more than three decades. Pick up a dashboard Jesus or a Frida Kahlo mesh bag. It has a great selection of comics, and in back is **La Luz de Jesus**, one of LA's top lowbrow art galleries. (☎323-663-0122; 4633 Hollywood Blvd, Los Feliz;

⌚11am-7pm Mon-Wed, 11am-9pm Thu-Sat, noon-6pm Sun; **M**Vermont/Sunset)

Driftwood VINTAGE

It doesn't have the largest vintage selection in Silver Lake, but it gets points for panache. Located near Café Stella (see 5 ❌ Map p44 D7), Driftwood's old-school desks and filing cabinets, Linda Ronstadt records, Princeton T-shirts, old worn leather boots and some new denim are all artfully arranged. (www.driftwoodla.com; 3938 W Sunset Blvd; ⌚noon-8pm Sun-Wed, 11am-9pm Thu-Sun; **P**; 🚌MTA 2)

Local Life
Echo Park

Getting There

🚗 **Car** Just west of Downtown, Sunset Blvd is the main thoroughfare. You may also access Echo Park from I-101.

🚌 **Bus** Metro bus lines 2/302 serve the district.

If you dig the uneasy interface of edgy urban art, music and culture in multi-ethnic neighborhoods, you'll love Echo Park, punctuated by the fountain lake featured in Polanski's *Chinatown*. Well, the artists and hipsters have arrived, but the *panaderias* and *cevicherias* remain mostly untouched.

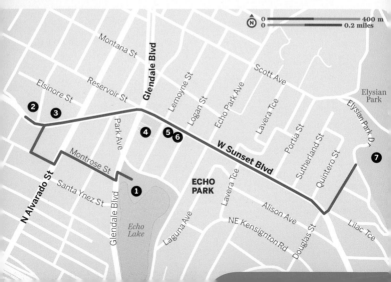

❶ Echo Park Lake

A former reservoir to homesteading families in the late 19th century, **Echo Park Lake** (www.laparks.org; 751 Echo Park Ave) is best known as the setting for Jake Gittis' surreptitious canoeing shenanigans in Polanski's classic film, and for its keyhole vistas onto Downtown LA's skyline. The lake was in municipal rehab at research time. But it should be newly planted with lotus blossoms and glittering visibly soon.

❷ I Am 8 Bit

Echo Park's funkiest art space, **I Am 8 Bit** (www.iam8bit.com; 2147 W Sunset Blvd; 1-8pm Thu, to 9pm Fri, noon-9pm Sat, noon-6pm Sun) offers stellar art shows at its expansive 4500-sq-ft gallery in the heart of Echo Park.

❸ Mohawk Bend

The owners of **Mohawk Bend** (213-483-2337; www.mohawk.la; 2141 W Sunset Blvd; dinner Mon-Fri, lunch & dinner Sat & Sun;), Echo Park's most upscale kitchen, took an old theater, blew it up and created a soaring atrium where you'll dine on uplifted pub fare crafted from all-Cali ingredients.

❹ Night Music

Eastsiders hungry for an eclectic alchemy of sounds pack the **Echo** (www.attheecho.com; 1822 W Sunset Blvd; tickets $10-26;). It books indie bands like Black Rebel Motorcycle Club, and also has regular club nights in the larger Echoplex Theater.

❺ 826 LA

At first glance, the **Time Travel Mart** (www.826la.org; 1714 W Sunset Blvd; noon-8pm Mon-Fri, noon-6pm Sat & Sun) is a convenience store for time travelers, stocked with anything a time traveler might need. But it's really just a front for a drop-in tutoring and writing program, the brainchild of author and McSweeney's founder, Dave Eggers.

❻ Kind Kreme

Sage (310-456-1492; www.sagevegan bistro.com; 1700 W Sunset Blvd; lunch & dinner;) is an organic vegan kitchen with sandwiches and veggie burgers, crafted with love and talent and served in heaping portions. And the menu is the *second*-best thing here. The best? That would be **Kind Kreme's** (www.kindkreme.com) good-for-you, raw ice cream. Taste to believe.

❼ Dodger Stadium

Built in 1962, and one of Major League Baseball's classic ballparks, **Dodger Stadium** (866-363-4377; http://losangeles.dodgers.mlb.com/la/ballpark/tours.jsp; 1000 Elysian Park Ave; tours adult/child 4-14yr & senior $15/10; 10am & 11:30am;) is now offering regular behind-the-scenes tours through the press box, the Dodger dugout, the field and the Tommy Lasorda Training Center. Of course, the best way to experience it is to catch a ballgame.

Explore

West Hollywood & Beverly Hills

In West Hollywood, rainbow flags fly proudly over Santa Monica Blvd and the set-piece Sunset Strip is where Hollywood has mingled for decades. Of course, ever since Will Rogers founded it, Beverly Hills has been the standard-bearer of Angelino wealth and power. And there remains ample bling on her boulevards.

The Sights in a Day

☀ Breakfast at a Harvey Weinstein favorite, **Hugo's** (p60), then hike Runyon Canyon before it gets too hot. Afterwards, meander down to Melrose Ave to enjoy a long shop that starts off with a spiritual navel-gaze through the **Bodhi Tree** (p64), ventures into high end around **Diane von Furstenberg** (p66) and **Fred Segal** (p65), and ends in the dark-hearted kitsch of **Necromance** (p67). And don't miss MOCA's satellite gallery at the **Pacific Design Center** (p58).

☀ Order a bag lunch at **Ink Sack** (p65) if you have a taste for high-end hoagies, otherwise make your way to Beverly Hills for a Mediterranean lunch with a twist at **Momed** (p58), a stroll along **Rodeo Dr** (p64) and a digression into **Barneys** (p67).

☾ Begin with a cracked-ice cocktail at **Comme Ca** (p61), where the menu will likely be inviting, but if you manage to put off dinner consider a reservation at **Angeli Caffe** (p58) or **Bouchon** (p59). Now it's time to hit the Sunset Strip for timely music at the **Roxy** (p62) or **House of Blues** (p62). Then dance your ass off at **Trousdale** (p64) or **Hyde Lounge** (p63) before last call at **Bar Marmont** (p61).

 Best of Lost Angeles

Eating

Bouchon (p59)

Yakitoriya (p60)

Dan Tana's (p59)

Ink (p65)

Drinking

Bar Marmont (p61)

Comme Ca (p61)

Shopping

Barney's New York (p67)

Diane von Furstenberg (p66)

Fred Segal (p65)

Getting There

🚌 **Bus** MTA, LA's principal transit authority, connects West Hollywood with all other parts of town.

For reviews see

◉	Sights	p58
✕	Eating	p58
🍷	Drinking	p61
★	Entertainment	p63
🔒	Shopping	p65

A   B   C   D

1

0   1 km
0   0.5 miles

Greystone
Park

2

Doheny Rd   ★28

23 ★   **Sunset Strip**   Holloway Dr
🔒 34

Loma Vista Dr

N Sierra Dr

N Alta Dr

W Sunset Blvd

Cynthia St

🍷 21

West Knoll Dr

N La Cienega Blvd

Elevado Ave

31

15 ★

3

N Hillcrest Rd

N Maple Dr

9
✕
26 ★   30   18   *Pacific
Design
Center* 🅿   2 ◉ ⓘ   33 🔒   5 ✕

★   ✕   ★   🔒   **Melrose Ave**
Melrose Ave

Santa Monica Blvd

San Vicente Dr

Huntley Dr

Carmelita Ave

N Palm Dr

Beverly
Gardens
Park

Beverly Blvd

11 ✕

4

Civic Center Dr

N Elm Dr

N Palm Dr

N Oakhurst Dr

N Almont Dr

36
🔒

Alden Dr

W 3rd St

N La Cienega Blvd

Burton Way

7 ★

N Beverly Dr

Dayton Way

S Doheny Dr

S La Peer Dr

N Robertson Blvd

Colgate Ave

N Carson Rd

5

Rodeo Dr

32 🔒

**BEVERLY
HILLS**

8 ★

6 ✕

Clifton Way

🔒 43

Wilshire Blvd

N Rexford Dr

E

F

G

H

To Runyon 3
Canyon

25
17 29

W Sunset Blvd

1

De Longpre Ave

N Vista St
N Martel Ave
N Fuller Ave
N Formosa Ave

Fountain Ave

27

William
S Hart
Park

22

N Crescent Heights Blvd

N Gesesee Ave

Plummer
Park

Poinsettia Dr

16 13

2

12

N Flores St

Norton Ave

**WEST
HOLLYWOOD**

39 Norton Ave

Santa Monica Blvd

Santa Monica Blvd

19

Santa Monica Blvd

N Orlando Ave
N Kings Rd
N Sweetzer Ave

Romaine St

N Laurel Ave

N Fairfax Ave

N Orange Grove Ave
N Ogden Dr
N Genesee Ave
N Spaulding Ave
N Stanley Ave
N Curson Ave
N Sierra Bonita Ave
N Gardner St
N Vista St

Poinsettia
Recreation
Center

Warner
Hollywood
Studios

Willoughby St

Willoughby Ave

Waring Ave

Waring Ave

14 24

10

Melrose
Pl

1

40

Melrose Ave

35

Melrose
Ave

37

20

Melrose Ave

42 41

3

Clinton St

38

Clinton St

**MELROSE/
LA BREA**

**BEVERLY
CENTER
DISTRICT**

N Sweetzer Ave

Rosewood Ave

N Edinburgh Ave
N Hayworth Ave

N Ogden Dr

N Gardner St
N Vista St
N Martel Ave
N Fuller Ave
N Poinsettia Pl
N Alta Vista Blvd
N Formosa Ave
N Detroit St

Oakwood Ave

**FAIRFAX
DISTRICT**

4

Beverly Blvd

Beverly Blvd

Beverly Blvd

W 1st St

S Edinburgh Ave

**MID-
CITY**

The Grove

Pan
Pacific
Park

S Gardner St
S Vista St
S Martel Ave
S Fuller Ave
S Poinsettia Pl
S Alta Vista Blvd

W 1st St

4

S Orlando Ave
S Sweetzer Ave

W 3rd St

W 2nd St

Colgate Ave

S Fairfax Ave

The Grove Dr

W 3rd St

Colgate Ave

5

Sights

Melrose Ave
COMMERCIAL DISTRICT

 Map p56, F3

A popular shopping strip as famous for its epic people watching as it is for its consumer fruits. You'll see hair (and people) of all shades and styles, and goods from gothic jewels to custom sneakers to stuffed porcupines to Tiger Woods sex dolls. (Melrose Ave btwn Fairfax & La Brea; 🚌MTA 10/48)

Pacific Design Center
LANDMARK

 Map p56, D3

Inside the blue-and-green leviathan at the corner of Melrose and San Vicente – the 'Blue Whale' – are more than 100 interior showrooms for architecture and design pros. The **Museum of Contemporary Art** (MOCA; ☎310-289-5223) maintains a satellite gallery here with rotating design- and architecture-related exhibits. (www.pacificdesigncenter. com; 8687 Melrose Ave; ⏰9am-5pm Mon-Fri; 🚌MTA 10/48)

Runyon Canyon
HIKING

 Map p56, F1

A chaparral draped in the Hollywood Hills, this 130-acre public park is as famous for its beautiful, bronzed and buff runners as it is for the panoramic views from the upper ridge. (2000 N Fuller Av; ⏰dawn-dusk; 🚌MTA 217)

Eating

Son of a Gun
SEAFOOD **$$**

 Map p56, E5

If you are the sort who loves seafood, head straight for the kitchen that Details and Bon Apetit have both listed as top newcomers in 2011. It has a smoked Mahi dip, luscious salmon collars with yakitori glaze, a hangar steak plated next to fried oysters, and even alligator schnitzel. Hey, the owner-chefs are from Florida and got their start creating self-ascribed 'stoner food,' ie dreaming up dishes they wanted to eat. The menu changes daily, so don't be ashamed to come back for seconds. (☎323-782-9033; www.sonofagunrestaurant. com; 8370 W 3rd St; dishes $8-27 ; ⏰11:30am-2:30pm Mon-Fri, 6-11pm Sun-Thu, to midnight Fri & Sat; 🚌MTA 16/316, 218)

Comme Ca
FRENCH **$$**

 Map p56, D3

The dining is French bistro classic. Think: roasted meats (like lamb shank), *moules frites* and bouillabaisse, served in white leather booths beneath wafting jazz. Oh, and there's the bar. Cocktails simply do not get much better (see p61). (☎310-782-1178; www.comme carestaurant.com; 8479 Melrose Ave; dishes $8-28; ⏰lunch & dinner; P; 🚌MTA 10/48)

Momed
MEDITERRANEAN **$$**

 Map p56, A5

Yes, it has the traditional Mediterranean dishes covered, but it also melts

avocado into its hummus, crafts shawarma from duck breast, oven-dried
tomatoes and fig confit, and loads flat
breads with shredded *jidori* chicken,
Turkish apricots and spicy tomato
spread. (☎310-270-4444; www.atmomed.
com; 233 S Beverly Dr; dishes $5-24; ☺lunch
& dinner; 🚇MTA 14/37)

Nate 'n Al   DELI $$

7 🍴 Map p56, A5

Dapper seniors, chatty girlfriends, busy
execs and even Larry King have kept
this New York–style spot busy since
1945. We're partial to the pastrami,
made fresh on-site. (www.natenal.com; 414
N Beverly Dr; dishes $6.50-13; ☺breakfast,
lunch & dinner; 👶; 🚇MTA 14/37)

Bouchon   FRENCH $$$

8 🍴 Map p56, A5

Quiche and salad, oysters on the half
shell or mussels steamed opened in
white wine sauce, Thomas Keller's
newest branch of his Bouchon empire
brings you French bistro cuisine in
classy environs. (☎310-279-9910; www.
bouchonbistro.com; 235 N Cañon Dr; mains
$17-36; ☺lunch & dinner; P; 🚇MTA 14/37)

Dan Tana's   ITALIAN $$$

9 🍴 Map p56, C3

Three reasons the red booths of this
47-year-old exclusive, yet somehow
still laid-back, Italian chophouse
remain packed with Hollywood celebrities and athletes on a near nightly

Pacific Design Center (architect Cesar Pelli)

basis: the steaks, the service, and the hours. It serves late supper until 1:30am. (☎310-275-9444; www.dantanasrestaurant.com; 9071 Santa Monica Blvd; mains $ 22-29; ⏰5pm-1:30am; 🚇MTA 4)

M Café MACROBIOTIC $

10 Map p56, H3

Meals are mostly vegetarian and all macrobiotic, which means no meat and no refined sugar. It has seared tuna and wild salmon dishes, and plenty of tasty salads. (www.mcafedechaya.com; 7119 Melrose Ave; dishes $6-15; ⏰breakfast, lunch & dinner; 🅿🍴; 🚇MTA 10/48)

Dominick's CONTINENTAL $$

11 Map p56, D4

A rat pack staple when it opened in 1948, it has effortlessly held onto

---

Q Local Life
Grill Master

An easy 15-minute drive from Beverly Hills, **Yakitoriya** (☎310-479-5400; 11301 W Olympic Blvd, West LA; ⏰dinner; 🚻; 🚇BBB 4/5) is a chef-owned and family-operated *yakitori* (Japanese grilled chicken) joint that elevates simple grilled chicken skewers to unimaginable culinary heights. It's one of several tasty Japanese spots north of Olympic on Sawtelle. We love the wings, the neck, chicken skin, meatballs and the minced-chicken bowl topped with quail egg. It does livers, kidneys and hearts too.

---

that martini-era cool. The brick patio is a great spot for a long summer's dinner. The menu, mostly broiled and grilled seafood and steaks, is likewise understated yet satisfying. (☎323-652-2335; www.dominicksrestaurant.com; 8715 Beverly Blvd; dishes $8-38; ⏰dinner; 🅿; 🚇MTA 14/37)

Hugo's ORGANIC $$

12 Map p56, E2

Hugo's blipped onto the Hollywood radar in the early naughts when Harvey Weinstein was a morning regular and it became famous for the terrific frittatas and smoothies and a sustainability ethos. (www.hugosrestaurant.com; 8401 Santa Monica Blvd; ⏰breakfast, lunch & dinner; dishes $7-18; 🅿🍴; 🚇MTA 4)

Jones ITALIAN $$

13 Map p56, H2

Good food served late with a rock vibe and a pretty bar crowd. Slip into a booth, get the fried calamari, some kind of pizza, a beverage, and stick around awhile. (☎310-850-1726; 7205 Santa Monica Blvd; pizza & pasta $11-19; ⏰noon-2am Mon-Fri, 6pm-2am Sat & Sun; 🅿; 🚇MTA 4)

Village Idiot AMERICAN, PUB $$

14 Map p56, H3

Solid gastro-pub fare with great fish and chips and other comfort food for a smart but still plenty boisterous crowd. The kitchen stays open until midnight. Drinks flow until

2am. (☎323-655-3331; 7383 Melrose Ave; ⏰11:30am-midnight Mon-Thu, to 1am Fri & Sat; 🚇MTA 10/48)

Fresh East

ASIAN FUSION $$

15 🍴 Map p56, C3

The ingredients are healthy, locally sourced, mostly organic and delicious, and the retro design incorporates reused and recycled materials. The food formula: choose your protein and order it in a rice bowl, with noodles or in a Vietnamese-style baguette. (☎310-859-9989; www.fresheast.com; 8951 Santa Monica Blvd; mains $9-14; ⏰lunch & dinner; 🚇MTA 4)

Food Lab

MODERN AMERICAN $$

16 🍴 Map p56, H2

An easily ignored storefront opposite Warner Hollywood Studios, this cute deli offers gourmet sandwiches (think prosciutto and fig with ricotta on raisin walnut bread) and salads (we like the artichoke, tomato, edamame, green beans and hearts-of-palm concoction). (☎310-851-7120; www.foodlabcatering.com; 7253 Santa Monica Blvd; ⏰8am-8pm; 🚇MTA 4)

Drinking

Comme Ca

BAR

Here at Comme Ca (see 5 🍴 Map p56, D3) the brainy barstaff serve prohibition-era cocktails – meaning they only use what was available during the 1920s and 1930s. No tropical fruits and, as one particularly surly barman says,

Q Local Life
All Inked Up

Top Chef's inked-up Michael Voltaggio is the latest kitchen slave to parlay small-screen cult stardom (and a Michael Ovitz investment) into brick-and-mortar success. At research time, his **Ink** (Map p56, E3; ☎323-651-5866; www.mvink.com; 8360 Melrose Ave; ⏰8am-8pm; 🚇MTA 10/48) was the toughest reservation to get in town. If you can't bear to run the reservation gauntlet there is always the **Ink Sack** (Map p56, E3; www.mvink.com; 8360 Melrose Ave; sandwiches $4-6; ⏰11am-4pm Wed-Sun; 🚇MTA 10/48), where Voltaggio stuffs four-inch baguettes with cold fried chicken, pork belly and Korean barbecue short rib.

'no fucking cranberry juice.' The Made in Mexico mixes tequila, muddled lime and mint, finished with sliced cucumber. (www.commecarestaurant.com; 8479 Melrose Ave; ⏰5:30-11pm; **P**; 🚇MTA 10/48)

Bar Marmont

BAR

17 🍺 Map p56, F1

Elegant, but not stuck up. Been around, yet still cherished. With high ceilings, molded walls and terrific martinis the famous and wish-they-weres still flock here. If you time it right you might see Thom Yorke or, perhaps, Lindsey Lohan. Come here during the week. Weekends are for amateurs. (🖀323-650-0575; 8171 Sunset Blvd; ⏱6pm-2am; 🅿; 🚇MTA 2)

Abbey
BAR

18 🍷 Map p56, C3

Since its opening more than 20 years ago as a tiny local coffee shop, the Abbey has expanded five times to its present incarnation as restaurant, bar and nightclub, complete with patios, cabanas and lounges peopled with an open, sexually diverse West Hollywood crowd. (🖀310-289-8410; www. abbeyfoodandbar.com; 692 N Robertson Blvd; ⏱8am-2am; 🚇MTA 4)

Bar Lubitsch
BAR

19 🍷 Map p56, G2

Would you seriously consider venturing into the Russian wing of West Hollywood and leave without sipping potato vodka? This spare yet stylish brick house of a vodka bar will keep you lubricated. (www.barlubitsch.com; 7702 Santa Monica Blvd; ⏱6pm-2am Mon-Fri, 8pm-2am Sat & Sun; 🅿; 🚇MTA 4)

Foundry
LOUNGE

20 🍷 Map p56, G3

Live jazz and absinthe, anyone? Granted the layout ain't winning any design awards, but why not patronize a place that brings in live bands regularly, jazz combos every Thursday night, and when absinthe is the cocktail of choice? The music rolls on from 9:30pm to 1am and it's free. (🖀www. thefoundryonmelrose.com; 7465 Melrose Ave; ⏱5:30pm-2am; 🚇10/48)

Palms
BAR

21 🍷 Map p56, D2

This staple has been keeping lesbians happy for more than three decades and even gets the occasional celebrity drop-in, as in Melissa Etheridge or Ellen DeGeneres. Beer is the beverage of choice and the Beer Bust Sundays are perfect for those who don't want the weekend to end. (www.thepalmsbar. com; 8572 Santa Monica Blvd; ⏱8pm-2am Mon-Sat, from 6pm Sun; 🚇MTA 4)

DAV D PEEVERS/LONELY PLANET IMAGES ©

Abbey

Entertainment

House of Blues
LIVE MUSIC

22 ⭐ Map p56, E1

Despite a Disneyfied 'Mississippi blues shack' exterior, this center-of-the-strip music hall books quality, sometimes quirky, small-venue bands from all over the US and abroad. You can sometimes glimpse big names up close here. (☎323-848-5100; www.hob.com; 8430 W Sunset Blvd; **P**; ⬚MTA 2)

Roxy
LIVE MUSIC

23 ⭐ Map p56, C2

A Sunset fixture since 1973, the Roxy has presented everyone from Miles Davis to David Bowie to Janes Addiction, was central to John Lennon's famous Lost Weekend in 1975, and still occasionally manages to book music that matters. (www.theroxyonsunset.com; 9009 W Sunset Blvd; ⬚MTA 2)

Groundlings
COMEDY

24 ⭐ Map p56, H3

An improv school and company that launched Lisa Kudrow, Will Ferrell, Maya Rudolph and other top talent. On Thursdays the main company, alumni and surprise guests riff together in *Cookin' with Gas*. (www.groundlings.com; 7307 Melrose Ave; tickets $14-18; ⬚MTA 10/48)

Book Soup

Hyde Lounge

CLUB

25 Map p56, F1

Another in SBE's growing pantheon of
nightclubs, this one has been quietly
drawing an A-list-speckled crowd
for years. Mondays and Saturdays
are best, but make arrangements in
advance to slip by the door masters.
(☎323-525-2444; www.sbe.com/hyde.com;
8029 Sunset Blvd; ⊙6pm-2am Wed-Sat;
☒MTA 2)

Troubadour

LIVE MUSIC

26 Map p56, C3

A mix of rock legends, cult favorites
and web-launched up-and-comers
haunt this legendary rock hall – open
since 1957. Big-timers like Bob Dylan,
Joni Mitchell, James Taylor and

Guns N' Roses played early gigs here.
(☎310-276-6168; www.troubadour.com;
9081 Santa Monica Blvd; ☒MTA 4)

Comedy Store

COMEDY

27 Map p56, E1

Sammy and Mitzi Shore's famous
stage. Sammy launched the club, but
Mitzi was the one who brought in hot
young comics like Richard Pryor and
George Carlin. These days, Pauly runs
it, and battle-tested comics still prowl.
(www.thecomedystore.com; 8433 W Sunset
Blvd; ℗; ☒MTA 2)

Trousdale

CLUB

28 Map p56, B2

The first Brent Bolthouse joint since
he went indie. Think of a Mafioso rec

room and fill it with the scantily clad, well coiffed and comely. (www.trousdale lounge.com; 310-274-7500; 9229 W Sunset Blvd; **P**; **MTA 2**)

Laugh Factory
COMEDY

29 Map p56, F1

The Marx Brothers used to keep offices at this long-standing club with multicultural programming, including the often hilarious Chocolate Sundays and Latino Night. It's mostly up-and-comers here, but they do get some big names. Kevin Nealon had a residency at research time. (www.laughfactory.com; 8001 W Sunset Blvd; **P**; **MTA 2**)

Factory/Ultra Suede Gay CLUB

30 Map p56, C3

This giant, sexually ambivalent double club has an edgy New York feel. On Friday night, the Girl Bar (at Ultra Suede) is the preferred playground of fashion-forward femmes, while abdo-men strut their stuff on Saturdays. (www.factorynightclub.com; 652 La Peer Dr; **MTA 4**)

Micky's
GAY CLUB

31 Map p56, C3

Recently reopened after a fire, Micky's is the quintessential WeHo dance club, with go-go boys, expensive drinks, attitude and plenty of eye candy. (www.mickys.com; 8857 Santa Monica Blvd; **MTA 4**)

Shopping

Rodeo Drive
SHOPPING DISTRICT

32 Map p56, A5

It's pricey and pretentious, but no trip to LA would be complete without a saunter along Rodeo Dr, the famous three-block ribbon of style where sample-size fembots browse for **Escada** (www.escada.com; 250 N Rodeo Dr) and **Prada** (www.prada.com; 343 N Rodeo Dr). The latter's flagship store at No 343 is a Rem Koolhaas–designed stunner lidded by a pitched-glass roof.

Bodhi Tree
BOOKS

33 Map p56, D3

Here since 1970, this cozy cottage of enlightenment carries an impressively broad range of spiritual-minded books – Buddhism, Christianity, astrology, shamanism – that's attractive to students and dabblers alike. Psychic readings offered daily. (310-659-1733; www.bodhitree.com; 8585 Melrose Ave; 10am-11pm; **MTA 10/48**)

Book Soup
BOOKS

34 Map p56, C2

Art, film and California travel are especially strong at this literary indie landmark in the heart of Sunset Strip. Author appearances range from Ron Jeremy to David Mamet to *Californication's* Hank Moody. (310-659-3110; www.booksoup.com; 8818 W Sunset Blvd; 9am-10pm, newsstand 10am-6pm; **P**; **MTA 2**)

Fred Segal BOUTIQUE

35 Map p56, F3

Several high-end boutiques cluster under this one impossibly chic but slightly snooty roof. Celebs circle for the latest from Costume National, Missoni, and Rag and Bone, while those in the know (including savvy stars) arrive early for deep discounts at the September sale. (☎323-651-4129; www.fredsegalcouture.com; 8100 Melrose Ave; ⏰10am-7pm Mon-Sat, noon-6pm Sun; P; 🚇MTA 10/48)

Kitson WOMEN'S CLOTHING

36 Map p56, C4

Follow the fun, funky and fab to this green-and-white pop tart where moneyed sceney-boppers flock for up-to-the-second fashion. For fashion-forward families there's also **Kitson Men** (146 N Robertson Blvd) and **Kitson Kids** (108 S Robertson Blvd). (☎310-859-2652; www.shopkitson.com; 115 S Robertson Blvd; ⏰10am-7pm Mon-Fri, 9am-7pm Sat, 11am-6pm Sun; 🚇MTA 16/316)

Melrose Trading Post VINTAGE, GIFTS

37 Map p56, F3

Young Hollywood loves snapping up trendy retro threads, jewelry, house wares and other offbeat items proffered by more than 100 purveyors. It's held every other Sunday in the Fairfax High parking lot, and proceeds help fund school programs. (www.melrosetradingpost.org; 7850 Melrose Ave; ⏰9am-5pm

Barneys New York

every 2nd and 3rd Sun of the month; 🚇MTA 10/48)

Slow VINTAGE

38 Map p56, G3

Worth a stop for vintage shoppers. There are specs and hats, sun dresses from the '60s, bandleader coats and ragged old army threads. It specializes in one-of-a-kind pieces and leather goods. Prices are reasonable. (www.slow7474.com; 7474 Melrose Ave; 🚇MTA 10/48)

Pleasure Chest EROTICA

39 Map p56, G2

LA's kingdom of kinkiness is filled with sexual, ahem, hardware catering to every conceivable fantasy and fetish. Please, who doesn't need a penis beaker? Yeah, there's more of the naughty than the nice here. (www.the pleasurechest.com; 7733 Santa Monica Blvd, West Hollywood; ⏰10am-midnight Sun-Wed, 10am-1am Thu, 10am-2am Fri & Sat; 🚇MTA 4)

Agent Provocateur LINGERIE

 40 Map p56, F3

As sexy as it is expensive, you'll love the sweet and naughty burlesque sheers, lace and silks that will work quite well with those thigh-highs, and could potentially coexist with that sharp, studded bustier if, you know, the occasion calls for it. (www.agentpro vocateur.com; 7961 Melrose Ave; ⏰closed Sun; 🚇MTA 10/48)

Necromance GOTHIC

 41 Map p56, H3

On the shortlist for creepiest shop in LA, this is a gallery of all species postmortem. Here are stuffed bears and deer, albino peacocks and ravens. There are cases of human skulls (yeah, they're real), fishbowls of ostrich vertebrae, vintage prosthetics, mutilated mannequins and, gasp, T-shirts! (📞323-934-8684; www.necromance. com; 7222 Melrose Ave; ⏰noon-7pm; 🚇MTA 10/48)

Munky King VINTAGE

42 Map p56, H3

A quirky dope Japan-imation gallery and toy store. It specializes in *omi* –

mountable toys with strange faces, and something of a totem for the new techno age. (www.munkyking.com; 7308 Melrose Ave; ⏰noon-7pm; 🚇MTA 10/48)

Barneys New York DEPARTMENT STORE

43 Map p56, A5

When Vince and his entourage went shopping together (and, seriously, how butch is that?), they explored these four floors of chic. (www.barneys.com; 9570 Wilshire Blvd, Beverly Hills; ⏰10am-7pm Mon-Wed, Fri & Sat, 10am-8pm Thu, noon-6pm Sun; 🅿)

Top Sights
Getty Center

Getting There

🚗 **Car** The Getty Center is best accessed from the I-405, exit Getty Center Dr.

🚌 **Bus** You can also take the bus (Metro 761), which stops at the main gate.

In its billion-dollar in-the-clouds perch, high above the city grit and grime, the Getty Center presents triple delights: a stellar art collection (Renaissance to David Hockney), Richard Meier's cutting-edge architecture (you'll love the jutting, cut-limestone bricks) and the visual splendor of seasonally changing gardens. On clear days, you can add breathtaking views of the city and ocean to the list.

Getty Center exterior

Don't Miss

Central Garden
More than a few visitors spend more time outside the museum's hallowed halls than inside, thanks to the magnificent, Robert Irwin–designed central garden. The 134,000-sq-ft design includes a stream that winds through and past 500-plus plant varieties that twist into a labyrinthine swirl.

Permanent Collection
Although not everyone is captivated by the Getty's collection of European art, which spans the 17th to 20th centuries, there are some gems. Pieces from the Baroque period can be found in the east pavilion, the west pavilion features Neoclassical and Romantic sculpture and decorative arts, while the north pavilion is stuffed with Medieval and Renaissance pieces.

Rotating Exhibitions
Of course, if moldy old Euro art bores you, you'll almost certainly find something edgy and contemporary floating through on an exhibition basis. At research time the center hosted a retrospective of LA painting and sculpture from 1950 to 1970 as part of the citywide Pacific Standard Time initiative, while upcoming photography exhibits in mid-2012 include the work of Herb Ritts, and *Photography and the Cult of Celebrity*, which extends from 1840 to the 1990s.

www.getty.edu

1200 Getty Center Dr

admission free; parking $15, free after 5pm

⊙10am-5:30pm Tue-Fri & Sun, to 9pm Sat

☑ Top Tips

▸ A great time to visit is in the late afternoon after the crowds have thinned.

▸ Children can take a Family Tour, visit the interactive Family Room, borrow a kid-oriented audio guide or browse the special kid bookstore.

✕ Take a Break

Downtown Beverly Hills is 15 minutes from the Getty Center, and it happens to be home to LA's best Jewish deli, **Nate 'n Al** (☎310-274-0101; www.natenal.com; 414 N Beverly Dr; ⊙7am-9pm), and arguably its best Mediterranean kitchen, Momed (p58).

Explore

Miracle Mile & Mid-City

The amorphous area we have called Mid-City encompasses the uber-groovy Fairfax District, once the domain of LA's Jews who moved here after WWII (along with Canters deli) from Boyle Heights, Miracle Mile with Museum Row, and old-money Hancock Park with its grand mansions. This is where LA's history (or even pre-history) and its on-rushing, creative, entrepreneurial future collide.

The Sights in a Day

☼ Enjoy a pastry and a coffee at **Joan's On Third** (p80), before making a beeline to **LACMA** (p74) to explore the newly redesigned campus. It will take hours to explore the permanent collections, rotating exhibitions and installations, so take your time. If the kids get bored stroll them over to the gooey **La Brea Tar Pits & Page Museum** (p72), where an excavation is underway, or if they're into cars, walk across the street to the **Petersen Automotive Museum** (p78).

☼ Grab a New American lunch at **Ray's** (p80) or graze among the **Food Trucks** (p81) on Wilshire Blvd. Families should head up Fairfax to the **Grove** (pictured left; p84) and the original **Farmers Market** (p81), for snacks and gifts. Hipsters will appreciate the stylings of **American Rag Cie** (p85) on La Brea, and the stunning **Fahey/Klein Gallery** (p85).

☾ Dinner comes down to two choices: **Pizzeria Mozza** (p79) or Japanese – meaning **Ita Cho** (p79). Both are top of the charts and unforgettable. Grab craftsman tequila at **El Carmen** (p82), then watch a show at the **El Rey** (p83), **The Mint** (p83) or **Largo at the Coronet** (p82). Honor last call at the **Roger Room** (p82), then hit **Canters** (p81) for after-hours nourishment and eavesdropping.

Top Sights

La Brea Tar Pits & Page Museum (p72)

LACMA (p74)

♥ Best of Los Angeles

Eating

Joan's on Third (p80)

Pizzeria Mozza (p79)

Matsuhisa (p81)

Ita Cho (p79)

Gallery Gazing

Wall Project (p78)

Drinking

El Carmen (p82)

Roger Room (p82)

Getting There

🚌 **Bus** MTA, LA's principal transit authority connects Mid-City with all other parts of town.

🚌 **Bus** Santa Monica's Big Blue Bus is also a useful network to the Westside and downtown.

Top Sights
La Brea Tar Pits & Page Museum

Even if you're not a fan of the *Ice Age* animated film trilogy, you'll likely have a ball at the unique Page Museum, an archaeological trove of skulls and bones unearthed at La Brea Tar Pits, one of the world's most fecund and famous fossil sites. Thousands of ice age critters met their maker between 40,000 and 10,000 years ago in crude oil bubbling from deep below Wilshire Blvd. A life-size mammoth family outside the museum dramatizes their fate.

👁 Map p76, D4

www.tarpits.org

5801 Wilshire Blvd

museum adult/senior, student & 13-17yr/5-12yr/ under 5yr $7/4.50/2/ free, tar pits only free

🕓9:30am-5pm Mon-Fri, 10am-5pm Sat & Sun

🚍MTA 20

Sculpture outside the Page Museum

Don't Miss

Project 23

During the construction of LACMA's new underground parking complex, 16 new fossil deposits were discovered, including a nearly complete skeleton of an adult mammoth. Paleontologists at the Page Museum helped preserve the fossilized bones, creating 23 fossil blocks. In 2008 excavation began and the fossils are now on public view, while excavators work seven days a week with hand tools such as dental picks, chisels, hammers and brushes to preserve and clean their bounty.

Pit 91

Located just west of the Page Museum is the Pit 91 excavation site; before Project 23, this was the only active excavation site at Rancho La Brea during the past 40 years. Discovered during the 1913–15 excavations it was decided that this large cluster of fossils would be left as is as a 'showpiece.' Unfortunately, after reaching a depth of approximately 9ft the excavation site suffered repeated cave-ins and floods, and it was abandoned, with thousands of fossils still awaiting excavation. These days, Pit 91 is the site of the Project 23 excavations.

Page Museum Collections

While all the giddy paleontologists and curious visitors converge around Pit 91, don't forget that within the Page Museum itself are 3.5 million fossil specimens of over 10,000 individuals representing 600-plus species of prehistoric mammals (90% of which were carnivores), birds (one of the largest collections of its kind in the world), flora, invertebrates, fish, amphibians and reptiles.

☑ Top Tips

▶ Although the museum does cost money, you can stroll through the park and admire the outdoor tar pits for free.

▶ The Rancho La Brea tar pit is well known for preserving the largest and most diverse collection of ice age plant and animal species ever discovered.

▶ Take your visit a step further and join one of the Page Museum's Family Overnight Trips, where the whole family can take part in fun educational games and activities and spend a night with the sabre-toothed tigers and woolly mammoths of the mind.

✕ Take a Break

Top off a visit to the Tar Pits with a meal at another family-friendly stopover, the original Los Angeles Farmers Market (p81). There's something here to satisfy even the fussiest mini-eaters among us.

Top Sights
LACMA

A recently completed, Renzo Piano–designed transformation has made the 20-acre Los Angeles County Museum of Art (LACMA) campus even sexier, and it was already LA's premier art museum. Here's an Aladdin's cave of paintings, sculpture and decorative arts stretching across ages and borders. Galleries are stuffed with all the major players – Rembrandt, Cézanne, Magritte, Mary Cassat, Ansel Adams and David Hockney, to name a few – plus several millennia's worth of global treasures.

⊙ Map p76, D4

www.lacma.org

5905 Wilshire Blvd

adult/senior & student/ under 18yr $15/10/free

⊙noon-8pm Mon, Tue & Thu, to 9pm Fri, 11am-8pm Sat & Sun

🚌MTA 20

Don't Miss

Japanese Art Pavilion

Pieces in this oh-so-Zen pavilion range in origin from 3000 BC to the 21st century. Here are Buddhist and Shinto sculpture, ancient ceramics and lacquerware, textiles and armor, and the epic Kasamatsu Shiro woodblock print, *Cherry Blossoms at Toshogu Shrine*.

Modern Art Collection

LACMA's permanent modern art collection is no slouch. Masterworks from luminaries like Picasso, Pissaro, Miro, Matisse, Magritte and Kandinsky are all here; some of them are from the recently acquired Janice and Henri Lazarof Collection.

Rotating Exhibitions

In addition to its stellar permanent collections, LACMA rotates some fabulous special exhibitions. Recently it hosted a solo Tim Burton exhibit that had Tinseltown buzzing, a mid-career retrospective of Bronx-born artist Glenn Ligon, and a series of cathedrals brushed by Monet and Lichtenstein.

☑ Top Tips

▶ Short on cash? Visit on the second Tuesday of the month and you can have access to all collections and exhibits for free.

▶ Friday nights are all about jazz. Throughout the year, world-class jazz musicians hold court in the plaza starting at 6pm. The sound and vibe are magnificent.

▶ LACMA also hosts film premieres, retrospectives, public 'conversations' with heavyweights like Clint Eastwood and John C Reilly, and a series of live classic screenplay readings directed by Jason Reitman (*Up In The Air*).

✕ Take a Break

Once you pay the relatively steep admission, odds are you won't want to stray too far from campus when your stomach grumbles. Just step over to Ray's (p80) for New American cuisine, or find a cheap and cheerful Food Truck (p81) across the street.

E F G H

N 0 — 1 km
0 — 0.5 miles

Melrose Ave

1

❌ 7

**MELROSE/
LA BREA**   Clinton St

N Sierra Bonita Ave
N Gardner St
N Vista St
N Martel Ave
N Fuller Ave
N Poinsettia Pl
N Alta Vista Blvd
N Formosa Ave
N Detroit St
N La Brea Ave
N Sycamore Ave

N Highland Ave
N Las Palmas Ave
N June St

Oakwood Ave

2

26
🔒

❌6
New
Beverly
Cinema

The Wilshire
Country Club

Beverly Blvd

24
☆

🔒
27

MID-CITY

Pan
Pacific
Park

S Gardner St
S Vista St
S Martel Ave
S Fuller Ave
S Poinsettia Pl
S Alta Vista Blvd
S Formosa Ave
W 1st St

S Orange Dr
S Mansfield Ave
S Citrus Ave
N Highland Ave
N Mc Cadden P.
S Las Palmas Ave
S June St

3

🔒
29

W 2nd St

W 3rd St

**HANCOCK
PARK**

S Alta Vista Blvd
S Sycamore Ave
W 4th St

S McCadden Pl

4

W 6th St

S La Brea Ave

W 6th St

21
☆

Craft & Folk
Art Museum

S Ridgeley Dr
S Dunsmuir Ave
S Cochran Ave
S Cloverdale Ave
S Detroit St

Wilshire Blvd

S Orange Dr
S Mansfield Ave
S Citrus Ave

15
❌

For reviews see	
🔵 Top Sights	p72
⦿ Sights	p78
❌ Eating	p79
🟢 Drinking	p82
☆ Entertainment	p82
🔒 Shopping	p84

5

Sights

Petersen Automotive Museum

MUSEUM

 1 Map p76, D5

Cars get their due at this four-story ode to the auto. Wander past a 1903 Cadillac, a 1923 UPS truck and the latest Bugatti – from zero to 60 in 2.5 seconds – as well as accessible displays fascinating for know-it-alls and newbies alike. Parking costs $8. (☎323-930-2277; www.petersen.org; 6060 Wilshire Blvd; adult/senior/student/5-12yr $10/8/5/3; ☺10am-6pm Tue-Sun; ☒MTA 20)

CBS Television City

STUDIO

 2 Map p76, D2

Here's where game shows, talk shows – including the always biting and fun *Real Time With Bill Maher* – and soap operas are taped, often before a live audience (☎323-575-2458 for tickets). (www.cbs.com; 7800 Beverly Blvd; **P**; ☒MTA 14/37)

Craft & Folk Art Museum

MUSEUM

 3 Map p76, D5

Zulu ceramics, Japanese *katagami* paper art, Palestinian embroidery – cultural creativity takes countless forms at this well-respected museum. The gift store is one of the best in town. (www.cafam.org; 5814 Wilshire Blvd; adult/student & senior/child under 10yr $7/5/free, 1st Wed of month free; ☺11am-5pm Tue-Fri, noon-6pm Sat & Sun; ☒; ☒MTA 20)

Wall Project

MUSEUM

 4 Map p76, D5

Some rather artistic slabs of the old Berlin Wall are on display on the lawn of a Wilshire high-rise across the street from LACMA as part of the global Wall Project. The images are evocative, but it's the feeling you won't be able to shake. (www.wallproject.org; 5900 Wilshire Blvd; ☒MTA 20)

A+D Museum

MUSEUM

 5 Map p76, D5

A small Getty-sponsored museum that keeps the finger on the pulse of emerging trends, people and products in the design and architecture community from its new base near the Petersen Automotive Museum. (☎323-932-9393; www.aplusd.org; 6032 Wilshire Blvd; adult/senior & student/child under 12yr

---

Understand
Hancock Park

There's nothing quite like the old-money mansions flanking the tree-lined streets of Hancock Park, a genteel neighborhood roughly bounded by Highland, Rossmore, Melrose and Wilshire. LA's founding families, including the Dohenys and Chandlers, hired famous architects to build their pads in the 1920s, and to this day some celebrities, including Kiefer Sutherland, make their homes here.

Exhibit at the Petersen Automotive Museum

$10/5; ⊘11am–5pm Tue–Fri, noon–6pm Sat & Sun; ◻MTA 20)

Eating

Ita Cho
JAPANESE $$$

6 Map p76, F2

Simply put, some of the best Japanese available in Los Angeles, which places it high in the running for tastiest nationwide. Don't miss the *nasu miso* (eggplant coated in sweet miso sauce), the buttery *enoki,* the broiled *unagi,* and anything sashimi. (☎323-938-9009; www.itachorestaurant.com; 7311 Beverly Blvd; ⊘lunch Mon–Fri, dinner Mon–Sat; P; ◻14/37)

Pizzeria Mozza
PIZZA $$$

7 Map p76, G1

An addictive pizzeria from the culinary minds of Nancy Silverton and Mario Batali. The fennel sausage, prosciutto and salami are indicative of the high-fat, high-taste toppings that gourmands and groupies demand. Equally packed is **Osteria Mozza**, the pizzeria's adjacent and much fancier sister venture. (☎323-297-0101; www.pizzeriamozza.com; 641 N Highland Ave; ⊘noon–midnight; ❢; ◻MTA 10/48)

Terroni
ITALIAN $$

8 Map p76, D2

Traditional Southern Italian cuisine, by way of, um… Toronto? Facts is facts, and you will love the *Carpaccio di tonno* and the *calamari alla griglia*. The thin-crust pizzas and pasta dishes are likewise fantastic. No substitutions tolerated! (☎323-954-0300; www. terroni.ca; 7605 Beverly Blvd; ⏰lunch & dinner; 🚊14/37)

Joan's on Third
GOURMET MARKET & DELI **$$**

9 🍴 Map p76, B3

One of the first market cafes in the LA area is still the best. The coffee and pastries are absurdly good. The deli churns out tasty gourmet sandwiches and salads and the recent expansion has just meant more fresh-baked, thinly sliced flavor. (☎323-655-2285; www.joansonthird.com; 8350 W 3rd St; ⏰8am-8pm Mon-Sat, to 6pm Sun; 🥗; 🚊MTA 16)

AOC
MEDITERRANEAN TAPAS **$$$**

10 🍴 Map p76, C3

Stylish AOC glows like the cozy wine cellar of a very good, very rich friend. It has over 50 wines by the glass, a three-page list of savory tapas and a welcoming but discreet vibe. Reservations recommended. (☎323-653-6359; www.aocwinebar.com; 8022 W 3rd St; 🥗; 🚊MTA 16)

Campanile
CALIFORNIAN-FRENCH **$$$**

11 🍴 Map p76, F4

Owner-chef Mark Peel has been turning market-fresh ingredients into beautiful dishes for over 15 years. Loyal locals mob the place on Mondays

Lunch at the Farmers Market

for $40 three-course dinners and on Thursdays for Grilled Cheese Night. (☎323-938-1447; www.campanilerestaurant. com; 624 S La Brea Ave; ⏰11:30am-2:30pm Mon-Fri, 6-10pm Mon-Wed, 5:30-11pm Thu-Sat, 9:30am-1:30pm Sat & Sun; 🚼; 🚊MTA 20)

Ray's
MODERN AMERICAN **$$**

12 🍴 Map p76, D4

LACMA's sleek, lauded new eatery offers updated versions of American classics like Shrimp n' Grits, and dreamy creations like mussels steamed in coconut, lime and chilli, and wild boar ravioli served in a glass box that spills onto LACMA's mod new plaza. (☎323-857-6180; www.patinagroup. com; 5905 Wilshire Blvd; ⏰lunch Mon-Fri, dinner Mon-Sat; P; 🚊MTA 20)

Matsuhisa
JAPANESE $$$

13 Map p76, A4

Long before he was a household name, chef Matsuhisa alchemized his imaginative, orgasmic cooked food in this kitchen. Robert De Niro couldn't live without it and together they opened Nobu in New York, and then things got all corporatey. (☎323-659-9639; www.nobumatsuhisa.com; 129 S La Cienega; ☺lunch Mon-Fri, dinner Mon-Sun; **P**; 🚇MTA 105)

Farmers Market
FARMERS MARKET $

14 Map p76, D3

There are more than 100 shops and stalls offering an international array of foods here, but the mouthwatering tacos at **Loteria Grill** (www.loteriagrill. com) and the spicy gumbo yaya at the **Gumbo Pot** (www.thegumbopotla.com) are our favorites. (☎323-933-9211; www.farmersmarketla.com; 6333 W 3rd St; ☺9am-9pm Mon-Fri, to 8pm Sat, 10am-7pm Sun; **P**🚲♿; 🚇MTA 16)

Umami Burger
BURGERS $

15 Map p76, F5

Although there are now five LA-area branches, this is where Japanese flavor (*umami* is Japanese for the fifth taste) and the American burger first collided. The namesake comes topped with a shitake 'shroom, oven-dried tomato, caramelized onions and a parmesan crisp. (www.umamiburger. com; 850 W S La Brea; ☺lunch & dinner; **P**; 🚇MTA 212, 20)

Canters
DELI $

16 Map p76, C2

This sprawling deli has been the late-night hangout of counterculturalists and rockers since the 1960s. Its dive bar, the **Kibitz Room**, once hosted regular Tuesday-night jams attended by luminaries like Jackson Browne and Slash (at the height of his fame). The deli fare is middling. The late-night scene is grand. (www.cantersdeli.com; 419 S Fairfax Ave; ☺24hr; **P**; 🚇MTA 217, 218)

Food Trucks
GLOBAL $

17 Map p76, D5

A convoy of LA's famed food trucks set up across from LACMA every weekday at noon to cater for the Wilshire Blvd lunch rush. You can get Indian at **New Delhi Express**, pho at **Phamish** (www. eatphamish.com) and Korean barbecue

 Local Life

Larchmont Ave

Who dropped Mayberry in the middle of Los Angeles? With its stroller-friendly coffee shops, locally owned boutiques and low-key patios, Larchmont is an oasis of square normality bordering a desert of Hollywood hipness. Gourmet sandwiches from **Larchmont Village Wine, Spirits & Cheese Shop** (☎323-856-8 www.larchmontvillagewine.com; 22 Larchmont Blvd; ☺10am-7pm Mo to 8pm Thu-Sat) are perfect for lywood Bowl picnic.

at **Bool** (www.roaminghunger.com/bool-bbq). There are usually more than a dozen options with meals for under $10. (Spaulding Ave & Wilshire Blvd; ⊙lunch Mon-Fri; ⊡MTA 20)

Drinking

El Carmen
TEQUILA BAR

 18   Map p76, C3

A pair of mounted bull heads and Lucha Libre (Mexican wrestling) masks create an over-the-top 'Tijuana North' look and pull in an industry-heavy crowd at LA's ultimate tequila and mezcal tavern (over a hundred to choose from). (8138 W 3rd St; ⊙5pm-2am Mon-Fri, 7pm-2am Sat & Sun; Ⓟ; ⊡MTA 16)

Roger Room
BAR

19   Map p76, A2

Cramped but cool. When handcrafted, throwback cocktails first migrated west and south from New York and San Fran, they landed here. Expect nothing but the best in speakeasy environs. (370 N La Cienega Blvd; ⊙6pm-2am Mon-Fri, 7pm-2am Sat, 8pm-2am Sun; Ⓟ; ⊡MTA 105)

Beverly Hills Juice Club
JUICE BAR

20   Map p76, B2

This hippie classic started out on Sunset when Tom Waits and Rickie Lee Jones used to stumble in between shows. It still attracts an in-the-know crowd craving wheatgrass shots and banana-manna shakes. Please, give

Hal our best. (8382 Beverly Blvd; ⊙7am-6pm Mon-Fri, 10am-6pm Sat; Ⓟ; ⊡MTA 14/37)

Entertainment

Largo at the Coronet
LIVE MUSIC

A long-time progenitor of high-minded pop culture (most recently they nurtured Zach Galifinakis to stardom), Largo at the Coronet (see **19** Map p76; A2) is based at the Coronet Theatre complex, and it's still bringing edgy comedy and nourishing night music to the people. (www.largo-la.com;

El Rey

366 N La Cienega Blvd; tickets $20-35; ⊙closed Sun)

El Rey LIVE MUSIC

21 ⭐ Map p76, F5

This is one gorgeous venue, an old art deco dance hall decked out in red velvet and chandeliers and flaunting an awesome sound system and excellent sightlines. Performance-wise, it's popular with indie bands and the rockers who love them. (www.theelrey. com; 5515 Wilshire Blvd; P; ☐MTA 20)

Mint LIVE MUSIC

22 ⭐ Map p76, A5

Built in 1937; legends like Ray Charles and Stevie Wonder played this intimate venue on the come up,

and recent classic Ben Harper started out here too. Expect a slate of terrific artists, sensational sound, and you'll never be more than 30ft from the stage. (www.themintla.com; 6010 W Pico Blvd; cover $5-18; P; ☐BBB 5)

Bang COMEDY

23 ⭐ Map p76, C2

Another improv and stand-up lab with a slate of classes and shows, and the occasional celeb cameo. Recent guest stars include Jeff Garlin (*Curb Your Enthusiasm*), Rainn Wilson (*The Office, USA*) and Sarah Silverman (*The Sarah Silverman Show*). (www.bang studio.com; 457 N Fairfax Ave; tickets $5-15; shows Thu-Sun; ☐MTA 217, 218)

Polkadots & Moonbeams

Acme Comedy Theatre COMEDY

24 ⭐ Map p76, F2

Not the most famous sketch and stand-up comedy theater, but big names like Adam Corolla, Joel McHale and Russell Brand have appeared and sometimes re-appear on stage. There are shows almost every weekend, but the calendar fills up haphazardly. (www.acmecomedy.com; 135 N La Brea Ave; tickets $10-15; shows most Thu-Sat; 🚌MTA 212)

Pacific Theatres at the Grove CINEMA

At the Grove (see **25** 🔒 Map p76, D3), this is a fancy all-stadium, 14-screen multiplex with comfy reclining seats, wall-to-wall screens and

superb sound. The Monday Morning Mommy Movies series (11am) gives the diaper-bag brigade a chance to catch a flick with their tot but without hostile stares from nonbreeders. (www.pacifictheaters.com; 189 The Grove Dr; adult/senior/child $12.75/8.75/9.50; 🚌MTA 16)

Shopping

Grove OUTDOOR MALL

25 🔒 Map p76, D3

This faux Italian palazzo is one of LA's most popular shopping destinations with 40 name-brand stores, a fountain, and a trolley rolling down the middle. (☎888-315-8883; www.thegrovela.com; 189 The Grove Dr; ⏱10am-9pm Mon-Thu, to 10pm Fri & Sat, 11am-8pm Sun; 🅿; 🚌MTA 16)

Remix Vintage SHOES

26 Map p76, E2

Feet feeling retro? Check out the never-worn vintage and reproduction footwear from the 1940s to '60s sold here. From baby-doll pumps to two-tone wingtips, your feet will be trippin' the light fantastic. (☎323-936-6210; 7605 Beverly Blvd; ☺noon-7pm Mon-Sat, to 6pm Sun; ☐MTA 14/37)

Fahey/Klein Gallery GALLERY

27 Map p76, F2

The best in vintage and contemporary fine-art photography by icons like Annie Leibovitz, Bruce Weber and the late, great rock-and-roll shutterbug, Jim Marshall. They even have his lesser-known civil rights catalogue in their vast archives. (www.faheykleingallery.com; 148 S La Brea Ave; ☺10am-6pm Tue-Sat; ☐MTA 212)

Polkadots & Moonbeams CLOTHING

28 Map p76, B3

Like a burst of sunlight on a cloudy day, this whimsical yet exceptional vintage women's-wear shop, stocked with affordable designer dresses, shades, scarves and hats, will make you smile. (www.polkadotsandmoonbeams.com; 8367 W 3rd St; ☺11am-7pm Mon-Sat, to 6pm Sun; ☐MTA 16)

American Rag Cie VINTAGE

29 Map p76, F3

This industrial-flavored warehouse-sized space has kept trend-hungry stylists looking good since 1985. Join them in their hunt for vintage leather, denim, tees and shoes. We particularly enjoyed the period homeware in the Maison Midi wing. (☎323-935-3154; 150 S La Brea Ave; ☺10am-9pm Mon-Sat, noon-7pm Sun; ☐MTA 212)

Known GALLERY

30 Map p76, C2

Casey Zoltan, a long-suffering, un-recognized artist, opened this special space to showcase his talents and the work of other underground, edgy modernists who blend various strands of the zeitgeist (like hip-hop, eastern mysticism, pollution and addiction) into art that is consistently arresting. (www.knowngallery.com; 441 N Fairfax Blvd; ☺noon-7pm Wed-Sat, to 6pm Sun; ☐MTA 217, 218)

Dope FASHION

31 Map p76, D2

This long block of Fairfax has long been considered a streetwear mecca, a place where hip-hop and skate culture harmonize, and this is the newest label to open shop. (www.dopecouture.com; 454 N Fairfax Blvd; ☺noon-8pm Mon-Sat, closed Sun; ☐MTA 217, 218)

Local Life
Culver City

Getting There

🚗 **Car** Culver City is accessible via Robertson Blvd from Mid-City and from Washington Blvd in Venice.

🚌 **Bus** The Culver City bus line serves areas in the city, Santa Monica, Venice and West LA.

A few years ago Culver City bloomed from its bland, semi-suburban studio-town roots into a stylish yet unpretentious destination for fans of art, culture and food, and it happened organically. Then the 2008 recession happened, and Culver City took a hit. But the roots of groovy stayed alive, and this 'hood has come back strong.

1 Blum & Poe

A major US art player and juggernaut of the Culver City arts district, **Blum & Poe** (www.blumandpoe.com; 2727 S La Cienega Blvd; ⊙10am-6pm Tue-Sat) reps international stars Takashi Murakami, Sam Durant and Sharon Lockhart.

2 Public Art

The Helms complex marks the beginning of Culver City's vital **Arts District** (www.ccgalleryguide.com; La Cienega btwn Venice & Washington), which runs east along Washington to La Cienega and up one block to Venice Blvd.

3 Something Strange

Arguably LA's most intriguing exhibition space, the **Museum of Jurassic Technology** (www.mjt.org; 9341 Venice Blvd; suggested donation adult/student & senior/child under 12yr $5/3/free; ⊙2-8pm Thu, noon-6pm Fri-Sun) has nothing to do with dinosaurs and even less with technology. Instead, you'll find madness nibbling at your synapses as you try to read meaning into mind-bending displays about Cameroonian stink ants and microscopic pope sculpture.

4 Gregg Fleishman Studio

Like Eames on acid, the **Greg Fleishman Studio** (www.greggfleishman.com; 3850 Main St; ⊙11am-7pm Wed-Sat) puts the 'fun' in functional with his ingenious solid birch plywood furniture

bent, carved and spiraled into springy forms. Lumbar support never looked or felt so...mind-opening.

5 Akasha & Ford's Filling Station

The kitchen at **Akasha** (☎310-845-1700; www.akasharestaurant.com; 9543 Culver Blvd; ⊙lunch & dinner Mon-Fri, dinner only Sat & Sun; 🖋🚻) takes all-natural ingredients and turns them into tasty small plates, such as bacon-wrapped dates stuffed with chorizo, and big ones like the zinfandel-braised short rib. And the 'Ford' in **Ford's Filling Station** (☎310-202-1470; www.fordsfillingstation.net; 9531 Culver Blvd; mains $11-30; ⊙lunch & dinner) in question is Ben Ford, and he'll fill you up in Culver City's original gastro pub. Flatbreads are toasted to perfection, the fish and chips have a tempura lightness, and the vegetarian polenta cake is a symphony of textures and flavors.

6 Kirk Douglas Theatre

An old-timey movie house has been recast as the 300-seat **Kirk Douglas Theatre** (www.centertheatergroup.org; 9820 Washington Blvd). Since opening in 2004, it has become an integral part of Culver City's growing arts scene, showcasing new plays by local playwrights.

Explore

Santa Monica

Here's a place where real-life Lebowskis sip White Russians alongside martini-swilling Hollywood producers. Where surf rats, skate punks, soccer moms, yoga freaks and street performers congregate along a sublime coastline, lapping at the heels of a chaparral-draped mountain range. Welcome to Santa Monica – LA's cute, alluring, hippie-chic little sister, its karmic counterbalance and, to some, its salvation.

The Sights in a Day

Enjoy breakfast at the beloved **Huckleberry** (p94), where the bakery is always rocking and the coffee is sublime. Then walk down Wilshire to the bluffs at **Palisades Park** (p93) and take it all in. Continue staring out to sea as you stroll south to the **Santa Monica Pier** (p89). If you have kids, hop the Ferris wheel at **Pacific Park** (p91). Otherwise walk to the end of the pier with the anglers, then down to the sand on **Santa Monica Beach** (p89), where you can stick your toes in cool Pacific blue or rent a bicycle or Rollerblades from **Perry's** (p91).

Granted, this whole commune with the sea thing could take all day, so, if your time is limited, double back to **Blue Plate Oysterette** (p94) for a tasty seafood lunch, then stroll and shop the **Third Street Promenade** (p98). As the afternoon grows late, make way to Main St and the **California Heritage Museum** (p93) then back to the beach for sunset.

Take your first beverage of the evening at the **Galley** (p96), and linger among the regulars for as long as you like. When dinner beckons, make your way to **Rustic Canyon** (p94), where the burgers and the wine are transcendent. If it's Wednesday, head to **Harvelle's** (p97) for the House of Vibe All-Stars. Otherwise, pile into the **Basement Tavern** (p96) on Main St.

Top Sights
Santa Monica Pier & Beach (p92)

Best of Los Angeles

Eating
Huckleberry (p94)

Real Food Daily (p95)

Sipping
Copa d' Oro (p97)

Shopping
Fred Segal (p99)

Sights
Jadis (p94)

Santa Monica Museum of Art (p93)

Getting There

Bus MTA, LA's principal transit authority, connects Santa Monica with all other parts of town.

Bus Big Blue Bus is the best choice for transport within Santa Monica, south to Venice and east to Westwood, and Downtown.

Top Sights
Santa Monica Pier & Beach

Dating back to 1908, the Santa Monica Pier is the city's most compelling landmark. There are carnival games, a vintage carousel, a Ferris wheel, a roller coaster and an aquarium, but the thing here is the view. Walk to the edge, lose yourself in the rolling blue-green sea or make your way to the golden sand that extends in a gentle arc for miles.

◉ Map p92, A3

www.santamonicpier.org

cnr Colorado Ave & Ocean Ave

admission free

⊙24hr

🚌BBB 1

Pacific Park, Santa Monica Pier

Don't Miss

Pacific Park

A small amusement park popular with kids, **Pacific Park** (☎310-260-8744; www.pacpark.com; per ride per person $3-5; 🚌BBB 1) has a solar-powered Ferris wheel, kiddie rides, midway games and food concessions. Check the website for discount coupons.

Original Muscle Beach

South of the pier is the **Original Muscle Beach**, where the Southern California exercise craze began in the mid-20th century, and new equipment now draws a new generation of fitness fanatics.

Beach Sports

Grab a bike, board, and a pair of blades or hit a beach-volleyball court and enjoy the beach like most Californians do, by getting active. **Perry's Café** (930 & 1200 Pacific Coast Hwy, 2400 & 2600 Ocean Front Walk) is the place to seek rentals. Its locations provide immediate access to the South Bay Bicycle Trail.

☑ Top Tips

▶ The pier comes alive with the Twilight Dance Series, a free concert program on summer Thursday nights. The lineup is generally eclectic and usually satisfying.

▶ A section of the South Bay Bicycle Trail runs along the beach – pick it up under the pier and ride all the way down to Redondo Beach if you're feeling strong.

▶ For cerebral pursuits, settle in at a first-come, first-served chess table at the International Chess Park, just south of the pier.

✗ Take a Break

Native Angelenos are familiar with the following summer pairing: Bay Cities (p95) sandwiches and the Santa Monica Beach. Here's what to do. Hit LA's best deli early (before the crowds become unmanageable) and tote your grub, beach blanket and beverages to the golden sand for a classic beach picnic.

Montana Ave

Palisades
Park

Idaho Ave

Washington Ave

California Ave

Ocean Ave

1st Ct
2nd St
3rd St
4th St
5th St
6th St

7th St

Lincoln Blvd

Wilshire Blvd

Palisades
Park

**SANTA
MONICA**

Arizona Ave

Santa Monica Blvd

9th St
10th St
11th St
12th St
14th St
15th St
16th St
17th St
18th St
19th St

Euclid St

Third St Promenade

Palisades Beach Rd

Santa Monica Visitor
Information Kiosk

Broadway

Santa
Monica
Place

Colorado Ave

To Bergamot
Station

Memorial
Park

Olympic Blvd

5th St

Main St

Santa Monica Fwy

Santa Monica
High School

Santa Monica
Bay

South Bay Bicycle Trail

Santa Monica
Visitors Center

Woodlawn
Cemetery

Pico Blvd
Bay St

Santa
Monica
College

Nielson Way

3rd St
4th St
6th St

Pearl St

Hollister Ave

0   500 m
0   0.25 miles

Barnard Way

Way

California Heritage
Museum

Jadis

Hill St

Ocean Park Blvd

Lincoln Blvd

2nd St
3rd St

Ashland Ave

Marine St

For reviews see	
◉ Top Sights	p90
◎ Sights	p93
✖ Eating	p94
🍷 Drinking	p96
★ Entertainment	p97
🛍 Shopping	p98

**Santa Monica
Pier & Beach**

14
2
27
25
7   9
22
17
19
26   24
30
5
6
8
12
13
29
1
10
20
11
18
16
3
28
15
4
23
21
30

Sights

Bergamot Station

ART

1  Map p92, D3

One of LA's best-known art nodes, this one-time trolley stop now houses 35 contemporary art galleries, the **Santa Monica Museum of Art** (☎310-586-6488; www.smmoa.org; ⊙11am-6pm Tue-Sat), a cafe and plenty of free parking on its 8-acre, campus-style complex. (☎310-453-7535; www.bergamotstation.com; 2525 Michigan Ave; admission free; ⊙10am-6pm Tue-Fri, 11am-5:30pm Sat; P; ☐BBB 5)

Palisades Park

PARK

2  Map p92, A2

Route 66, America's most romanticized byway, ends at this gorgeous cliffside park perched dramatically on the edge of the continent. This palm-dotted 1.5-mile greenway is tops with joggers and people-watchers, the ragged and the needy. (☎800-544-5319; southern terminus cnr Colorado Blvd & Ocean Ave; admission free; ⊙5am-midnight; ☝; ☐BBB 1)

California Heritage Museum

MUSEUM

3  Map p92, B5

For a trip back in time, check out the latest exhibit housed in one of Santa

LHB PHOTO/ALAMY ©

Palisades Park

Local Life

Annenberg Community Beach House

Like a beach club for the rest of us, this sleek and attractive public **beach club** (📞310-458-4904; www.beachhouse.smgov.net; 400 Pacific Coast Hwy; adult/child $10/4; ⏱8:30am-8:30pm Jun-Sep), built on actress Marion Davies' estate (she had a thing with William Randolph Hearst), has a lap pool, lounge chairs, yoga classes, beach volleyball, a fitness room, photo exhibits and even poetry readings. There's a cafe nearby, and it's set on a sweet stretch of Santa Monica Beach.

Monica's few surviving grand Victorian mansions – this one built in 1894. Curators present pottery, Craftsman furniture, folk art, vintage surfboards and other fine collectibles in dynamic fashion. (www.californiaheritagemuseum.org; 2612 Main St; adult/student & senior/child under 12yr $5/3/free; ⏱11am-4pm Wed-Sun; 🅿; 🚌BBB 1)

Jadis   MUSEUM

 4 🎯 Map p92, B5

A homespun museum crammed with old antique clocks, planes, globes, lights and gear madness – most of which were old film props. The prized piece is the robot from the famed 1927 film *Metropolis*. (2701 Main St; per person $1; ⏱noon-4pm Sun; 🚌BBB 1)

Eating

Rustic Canyon   CALIFORNIAN $$$

 5 🍴 Map p92, C2

Almost all the ingredients come from local organic producers, which means the menu shifts with availability, but count on two handmade pasta dishes, and an assortment of stunning small plates. And there is always the burger: a world-class mound of mouth-melting meat that eats like culinary soft porn. (📞310-393-7050; www.rucanyonwinebar.com; 1119 Wilshire Blvd; small plates from $12, mains $18-32; ⏱dinner; 🅿; 🚌BBB 2)

Huckleberry   CAFE $$

 6 🍴 Map p92, C2

Crostatas burst with fruit, bacon biscuits are glazed with maple, and pumpkin teacakes are spiced with ginger. Later in the day the crowds keep coming for the much-lauded barbecue pork sandwich, the brisket plate or any number of deli salads. We call it yuppie soul food. (www.huckleberrycafe.com; 1014 Wilshire Blvd; mains $9.50-13.50; ⏱breakfast, lunch & dinner; 🚌BBB 2; 🅿)

Blue Plate Oysterette   SEAFOOD $$

 7 🍴 Map p92, B2

There's only one reason to ignore a raw bar that includes a ceviche of the day, delectable oysters, prawns and clams – you've ordered the lobster roll or the lobster mac 'n' cheese. (📞310-576-3474; www.blueplatesantamonica.com; 1355 Ocean Ave; dishes $9-22; ⏱lunch & dinner; 🚌BBB 1)

Bay Cities
ITALIAN DELI **$**

8 Map p92, C2

Not just the best Italian deli in LA, this is arguably the best deli, period. With sloppy, spicy Godmothers (piled with salami, mortadella, *coppacola*, ham, prosciutto, provolone, and pepper salad) and tangy salads. Get your sandwich with the works. (www.baycitiesitaliandeli.com; 1517 Lincoln Blvd; sandwiches $4-12; 9am-7pm Tue-Sat, 9am-6pm Sun; P; BBB 3)

Sugarfish
SUSHI **$$**

9 Map p92, B2

The new Santa Monica shingle of LA's famed Sushi Nazi, aka Chef Nozawa. Don't suggest any menu editorials. Just mind your manners and eat what you're told to eat. It will be enlightening, and about half the price of his Valley location. (1345 2nd St; meals from $20; lunch & dinner; BBB 1)

Tacos Por Favor
MEXICAN **$**

10 Map p92, D3

This is a no-nonsense taco joint, a dingy hole-in-the-wall, smoky, hot, and crowded. It also happens to serve the best shrimp, chicken and *carne asada* tacos and burritos in town. Hence, the lunchtime crush. (1406 Olympic Blvd; mains from $6; breakfast, lunch & dinner; ; BBB 41)

Chinois
ASIAN FUSION **$$$**

Wolfgang Puck's Asian-fusion masterwork, Chinois, near Jadis (see 4 Map p92, B5), has been around since 1983, so it can (and does) seem dated, but you'll dig the open kitchen and stylish turquoise tabletops, and don't miss the sizzling catfish in ponzu sauce. (310-392-9025; www.wolfgangpuck.com; 2709 Main St; mains from $28; lunch Wed-Fri, dinner daily; P; BBB 1)

Le Pain Du Jour
FRENCH **$**

11 Map p92, C4

Flat out the best croissants and baguettes in LA, which is why this wholesale bakery makes its mint selling its goods to high-end restaurants throughout Southern California. The oozing almond croissant is a sweet, buttery path to gastro-enlightenment. (www.lepaindujour.com; 828 Pico Blvd Ste 2; pastries from $3; 7:30am-2pm; BBB 4, 7)

Real Food Daily
VEGAN **$$**

12 Map p92, B2

New World vegan cooking guru Ann Gentry gives meat and dairy substitutes an interesting inflection here. The lentil-walnut pâté is a complex starter, and classics like the Salisbury seitan (a wheat gluten–based dish) and tempeh tacos feed the body and soul. (www.realfood.com; 514 Santa Monica Blvd; mains $13-15; lunch & dinner; ; BBB 1)

Border Grill

MEXICAN $$

13 Map p92, B3

Dressed-up Mexican nouveau done to perfection, with four kinds of ceviche, and a terrific lamb tostada. Compared to most of LA's Mexican joints, it isn't cheap, but you get what you pay for here. (☑310-451-1655; www.bordergrill.com; 1445 4th St; mains $14-34; ☉lunch & dinner; ⬛BBB 1, 2, 3)

 Local Life

Farm Fresh

You haven't really experienced Santa Monica until you've explored one of the four weekly outdoor farmers markets stocked with organic fruits, vegetables, flowers, baked goods and fresh-shucked oysters. The Wednesday and Saturday **market** (Map p92, B2; www01.smgov.net/farmers_market; 3rd & Arizona; ☉9am-1pm Wed & Sat) is the biggest and arguably the best for fresh produce in all of LA, which is why it's so often patrolled by local chefs, but the **Sunday morning market** (Map p92, B5; 2612 Main St; ☉9am-1pm Sun) is more of a community scene with live music, pony rides, a half-dozen cooked-food stalls and a bicycle valet (um, yes, we know, but it is free). Relax with the locals on the luscious green lawn.

Father's Office

PUB $

14 Map p92, C1

This elbow-to-elbow gastropub is famous for its dry-aged-beef burger dressed in smoky bacon, sweet caramelized onion and an ingenious combo of Gruyère and blue cheese. Pair it with a handcrafted brew chosen from the three-dozen on tap. No substitutions tolerated. (1018 Montana Ave; ☉5pm-1am Mon-Thu, 4pm-2am Fri, noon-2am Sat, noon-midnight Sun; ⬛BBB 3)

Drinking

Basement Tavern

BAR, RESTAURANT

15 Map p92, B5

Tabbed as the 'best-kept secret on Main St,' this creative speakeasy, housed in the basement of the Victorian, is beloved for craftsman cocktails and a rich live-music calendar that features ragtime, New Orleans jazz and bluegrass bands. Enter around back. (2640 Main St; ⬛BBB 1)

Galley

BAR

16 Map p92, B4

A low-key, classic, nautically themed watering hole with strong drinks, icy martinis and a damned decent kitchen. Hence, the bachelor feed line at the bar. (www.thegalleyrestaurant.net; 2442 Main St; ⬛BBB 1)

Copa d'Oro LOUNGE

17 Map p92, B3

The gifted Vincenzo Marianella has trained a team to concoct addictive cocktails from a well of top-end liquors and a produce bin of fresh herbs and fruits. The rock tunes and smooth, dark ambience don't hurt. (www.copa doro.com; 217 Broadway; ⏰6pm-2am Mon-Fri, 8pm-2am Sat & Sun; 🅿; 🚇BBB 1)

Bar Chloe LOUNGE

Cozy, dark and elegant, with dangling chandeliers, twinkling candles, intimate booths, crisp white tablecloths, and a lavender gimlet that has earned rave reviews. Bar Chloe's (see 17 Map p92, B3) tapas and sliders are decent too. (www.barchloe.com; 1449 2nd St)

Flying Saucers COFFEE HOUSE

18 Map p92, B4

Small batches of locally roasted free-trade beans are ground, soaked and steamed into first-rate espresso drinks at this boho spot, where they serve *pain du jour* pastries and flaunt the works of local artists on the brick walls. (www.flyingsaucersla.blogspot.com; 312 Pico Blvd; 🅿; ⏰7am-5pm)

Entertainment

Harvelle's BLUES, JAZZ, FUNK

19 ⭐ Map p92, B3

Follow the sexy red glow and jazz-infused beats to cozy Harvelle's, way too cool for its 4th St, garage-adjacent digs. Wednesday night's House of Vibe act is absurdly funky and often features the unforgettable Chali 2na of Jurassic Five/Ozomatli fame. (📞310-395-1676; www.harvelles.com; 1432 4th St; ⏰8pm-2am; 🚇BBB 2)

McCabe's Guitar Shop ACOUSTIC

20 ⭐ Map p92, D4

This little guitar shop hosts some of the best small-venue shows around in its no-frills back room. Past bluegrass, folk and indie standouts include Ralph Stanley, Lucinda Williams and Gillian Welch. (📞310-828-4497; www. mccabes.com; 3101 Pico Blvd; shows $8-25; ⏰10am-10pm Mon-Thu, to 6pm Fri & Sat, noon-5pm Sun; 🚇BBB 7)

Zanzibar CLUB

21 ⭐ Map p92, B2

Beat freaks will be in heaven at this groovetastic den dressed in a sensuous Indian-African vibe with a shape-shifting global DJ line-up that goes from Arabic to Latin to African depending on the night. The crowd is just as multiculti. (www.zanzibarlive.com; 1301 5th St; cover $7-10; ⏰Tue-Sun; 🚇BBB 2)

Magicopolis MAGIC

22 ⭐ Map p92, B2

Aspiring Harry Potters (and their relatives) will enjoy the comedy-laced sleight-of-hand, levitation and other illusions performed by Steve Spills and cohorts in this intimate space.

There's even a small shop for all your wizard supplies. (🕿310-451-2241; www.magicopolis.com; 1418 4th St; tickets $24-29; ⏱8pm Fri & Sat, 2pm Sat & Sun; ♿; 🚇BBB 1, 2, 3)

Shopping

Planet Blue
FASHION

23 🔒 Map p92, B5

Everyone from moneyed hipsters to soccer moms to Hollywood royalty peruses the racks at this stylish boutique stocked with tremendous denim and contemporary casual collections, as well as high-end beauty essentials and some sexy silver too. There's also a location on Montana Ave. (www.shopplanetblue.com; 2940 Main St; 🚇BBB 1)

Paris 1900
VINTAGE

Paris 1900, near Jadis (see **4** ◉ Map p92, B5), hangs its rather stylish hats on its exquisite collection of vintage French fashion from 1900 to 1930, and a few new vintage-inspired garments. Expect the finest jewelry and lace with an emphasis on period bridal. Look for the Montmartre-inspired art nouveau entry. (www.paris1900.com; 2703 Main St; 🚇BBB 1)

Hundreds
URBAN

24 🔒 Map p92, B3

An LA-based, hip-hop-inspired label with terrific tailored T-shirts, hoodies, sweaters and jackets. It's all stylish

and affordable. (www.thehundreds.com; 416 Broadway Ave; 🚇BBB 1)

Third Street Promenade
MALL

25 🔒 Map p92, B2

Stretching for three long blocks, it offers carefree and car-free strolling and shopping accompanied by the sound of flamenco guitar or hip-hop acrobatics courtesy of street performers. (3rd St btwn Wilshire & Broadway; 🚇BBB1, 2, 3)

Santa Monica Place
MALL

26 🔒 Map p92, B3

The 'new,' but not really, mall at the south end of the Promenade recently had a reinvention that amounted to ceiling and wall removal, and an infusion of local flavor and corporate cash. Shops are posher than at the Promenade, and the dining deck is fabulous. (www.santamonicaplace.com; 395 Santa Monica Pl; ⏱10am-9pm Mon-Thu, to 10pm Fri & Sat, 11am-8pm Sun; 🚇BBB 1, 2, 3)

Hennessy + Ingalls
BOOKSTORE

27 🔒 Map p92, B2

With its sleek shelves, snappy organization and eye-catching titles, Hennessy + Ingalls is dedicated to art and architecture. It stocks everything from coffee-table books and fashion retrospectives to landscaping how-to tomes. (🕿310-458-9074; www.hennesseyingalls.com; 214 Wilshire Blvd; ⏱10am-8pm; 🚇BBB 2)

Puppetry at Whimsic Alley

Undefeated
SPECIALTY SNEAKERS

28 Map p92, B5

Sneaker-lovers camp outside this pint-sized store for the latest 'outside the box' styles from Nike, Converse, Vans and Adidas, each pair specially selected from the manufacturer by the manager. Word spreads online, and voilà, sidewalk campouts. (☎310-399-4195; www.undftd.com; 2654B Main St; ☺11am-7pm Mon-Sat, 10am-4pm Sun; ☒BBB 1)

Whimsic Alley
BOUTIQUE FOR MUGGLES, WIZARDS

29 Map p92, D2

Muggles love this magical store, where Harry Potter and friends seem to be waiting just a portkey away. Flip through Hogwarts sweaters and capes at Haber & Dasher, or find your wand at Phoenix Wands. (☎310-453-2370; www.whimsicalley.com; 2717 Wilshire Blvd; ☺11am-5pm Wed-Sun; ☒BBB 2)

Fred Segal
FASHION, JEWELRY

30 Map p92, B3

Celebs and beautiful people circle this impossibly chic but slightly snooty warren of boutiques that straddles 5th St and dominates an entire block. (www.fredsegalfun.com; 500 Broadway; ☺10am-7pm Mon-Sat, noon-6pm Sun; ℗; ☒BBB 1)

Top Sights
Malibu

Getting There

🚗 Car The I-10 be-
comes the California
Hwy 1 north in Santa
Monica. Follow it to
paradise.

🚌 Bus MTA's Malibu
Express line 534
leaves from Fairfax Ave
and Washington Blvd.

Everyone needs a little Malibu. Here's a moneyed,
stylish yet laid-back beach town and celebrity
enclave that rambles for 27 miles along the Pacific
Coast Hwy, blessed with the stunning natural
beauty of its coastal mountains, pristine coves, wide
sweeps of golden sand and epic waves, and lucky for
you, it's all just a drive away.

Don't Miss

Getty Villa

Getty Villa (www.getty.edu; 17985 Pacific Coast Hwy; parking $15; 🚊MTA 534) is an original Getty Museum set in a replica 1st-century Roman villa, and is a stunning 64-acre showcase for exquisite Greek, Roman and Etruscan antiquities amassed (legally and otherwise) by oil tycoon J Paul Getty.

El Matador State Beach

Arguably Malibu's most stunning beach, **El Matador** (32215 Pacific Coast Hwy; 🅿; 🚊MTA 534) is where sandstone rock towers rise from emerald coves, topless sunbathers stroll through the tides, and dolphins breech the surface beyond the waves. Spectacular.

Zuma & Westward Beach

Zuma (30000 Pacific Coast Hwy; 🅿; 🚊MTA 534) owns a blonde sweep of sand that has been attracting valley kids to the shore since the 1970s, but we prefer **Westward Beach** (6800 Westward Rd; 🅿; 🚊MTA 534), where rip currents can be strong but the water is crystal clear.

Surfrider Beach

Surf punks descend in droves to this point that shapes tasty waves. There are several breaks at **Surfrider** (Pacific Coast Hwy; 🅿; 🚊MTA 534). The closest is well formed for beginners; the others demand short boards and advanced-level skill.

☑ Top Tips

▶ It's best to explore Malibu midweek, especially in summer. That way you'll have the roads and the beaches mostly to yourself.

▶ Malibu is an ideal family destination. Kids can get busy getting dirty on the beach or in the hills, and mom can shop and celebrity-spot in the swanky shops off Cross Creek Rd.

▶ Parking on the PCH is free, and same goes for the road that links Zuma with Westward Beach, but if you park in a self-pay lot, make sure you pony up the cash or you will earn a fine.

✕ Take a Break

A Malibu favorite, **Café Habana** (📞310-317-0300; www.habana-malibu.com; 3939 Cross Creek Rd; ⊙lunch & dinner; 🅿🚻) does tacos, burritos and some Cuban classics like *ropa vieja* and a pulled-pork sandwich.

Explore

Venice

If you were born too late, and have always been a little jealous of the hippie heyday, come down to the boardwalk and inhale an incense-scented whiff of Venice, a boho beach town and long-time haven for artists, New Agers, road-weary tramps, freaks and free spirits.

The Sights in a Day

Line up with the bearded, sassy, disheveled masses at **Intelligentsia** (p110), and we mean literally line up, for what is arguably the best morning Joe in town. Sip it slowly as you stroll **Abbot Kinney Blvd** (p107), stepping into shops and galleries and becoming one with the artsy, boho vibe. Don't miss **Gebert Gallery** (p111), **Warakuku** (p112), **A + R Store** (p110) and **Alternative** (p110).

Lunch at **Joe's** (p108) before taking leave of Abbot Kinney, for now. Then wander down to the **Venice Canals** before heading for **South Venice Beach** and the **Venice Boardwalk** (p104) where you can watch the steroid-infused muscleheads get pumped at **Muscle Beach** (p105), spy interesting **graffiti** (p105) and watch the young punks tear it up at the **skate park** (p105). Relax with a drink at **Fig Tree's Café** (p110) and wait for the sun to drop along with the rest of the sinners and saints that make the boardwalk so...special.

After nightfall head to Rose Ave, where you can sip wine and nosh on charcuterie at **Venice Beach Wines** (p109), or opt for stellar draft beer and Mexi-fusion next door at **Oscar's Cerveteca** (p109). Then double back to Abbot Kinney, especially if it's a **First Friday** (p107) night, or even if it's a plain old Sunday or Monday when Hal's offers free live jazz.

 Top Sights

Venice Boardwalk (p104)

Best of Los Angeles

Eating
Gjelina (p107)

Abbot's Pizza Co (p108)

Joe's (p108)

Sipping
Venice Beach Wines (p110)

Shopping
Abbot Kinney Blvd (p107)

Getting There

🚌 **Bus** MTA, LA's principal transit authority, connects Venice with most other parts of town. Santa Monica's Big Blue Bus connects Venice with Santa Monica.

◉ Top Sights
Venice Boardwalk

Life in Venice moves to a different rhythm, and nowhere more so than on the famous Venice Boardwalk, officially known as Ocean Front Walk. It's a freak show, a human zoo, a twisted carnival, but as far as LA experiences go, it's a must. Encounters with budding Schwarzeneggers, hoop dreamers, a Speedo-clad snake charmer and a rollerskating Sikh minstrel jamming like Hendrix are almost guaranteed.

◉ Map p106, A3

Ocean Front Walk from Venice Pier to Rose Ave

admission free

⊘ 24hr

🚌 MTA 33, 333; BBB 2

Storefront on Venice Boardwalk

Don't Miss

Venice Beach Skate Park

Long the destination of local skate punks, the concrete has now been officially molded into the steel-fringed **Venice Beach Skate Park** (1800 Ocean Front Walk; ☉dawn-dusk; ☐BBB 1). Expect 17,000 sq ft of vert, tranny and street terrain with unbroken ocean views. The old-school-style skate run and the world-class pool are most popular for spectators.

Muscle Beach

Gym rats with an exhibitionist streak can get a tan and a workout at **Muscle Beach** (www.muscle beach.net; 1800 Ocean Front Walk; per day $10; ☉8am-7pm May-Sep, 8am-6pm Oct-Apr; ☐BBB 1), the famous out-door gym right on the boardwalk where Arnold once bulked up.

Graffiti Park

Venice Beach has long been associated with street art, and for decades there was a struggle between outlaw artists and law enforcement. Alas, art won out and now the **Venice Beach Graffiti Park** (1800 Ocean Front Walk; ☉dawn-dusk; ☐BBB 1), a conglom-eration of tagged-up towers and a freestanding concrete wall near the skate park, are forever open to aerosol Picassos.

☑ **Top Tips**

▶ During the summer the boardwalk is always alive. Off-season, there is still life around sunset when crowds gather at cafes and bars and on the bike path.

▶ The Sunday-afternoon drum circle draws hundreds of revelers for tribal jamming and spontaneous dancing on the grassy mounds beyond the skate park year-round.

▶ South of the Venice Pier at Washington Blvd, the throng dissipates, and the golden sands unfurl in a more pristine manner. Waves roll in consistently and are ideal for bodysurfing, and volleyball games tend to erupt at a mo-ment's notice.

✗ **Take a Break**

If you're in need of a psychic shower, head to the groovy cafes and galleries on upscale, yet still boho, Abbot Kinney Blvd.

A

0   400 m
0   0.2 miles

Santa Monica State Beach

11 ✕

Venice Beach

7 ✕
6 ✕

VENICE

◉ **Venice Boardwalk**

Ⓟ

Ocean Front Walk

Pacific Ave

Main St

Hampton Dr

Mildred Ave

Venice Way

Dell Ave

Grand Blvd

Abbot Kinney Blvd

Westminster Ave

San Juan Ave

Market St

Windward Ave

Santa Monica Bay

South Venice Beach

Ocean Front Walk

Canal Park

Venice Canals

Dell Ave

Venice Way

N Venice Blvd
S Venice Blvd

Washington Blvd

3rd St

4th St

5th Ave

Abbot Kinney Blvd

1 ◉ ✕ 4
3 ✕
14 🔒
17 🔒
16 🔒
18 🔒
15 🔒

Electric Ave

Rose Ave

9 ✕

Sunset Ave

Vernon Ave

Indiana Ave

Brooks Ave

Broadway

Westminster Ave

San Juan Ave

Santa Clara Ave

12 🍷
5 ✕
2 ✕
13 🍷

19 🔒
8 ✕

Electric Ave

California Ave

7th Ave

Lincoln Blvd

10 ✕

Ⓟ

For reviews see	
◉ Top Sights	p104
◉ Sights	p107
✕ Eating	p107
🍷 Drinking	p110
🔒 Shopping	p112

Sights

Abbot Kinney Boulevard
SHOPPING & GALLERY DISTRICT

1 Map p106, B2

The impossibly hip and beautiful mile-long stretch of Abbot Kinney Blvd between Venice Blvd and Main St is chock-a-block with unique boutiques, galleries, lofts, vintage clothing stores and sensational restaurants. (www.abbotkinney.org; Abbot Kinney Blvd; 🚌 MTA 33)

Eating

Gjelina
ITALIAN $$$

2 ✂️ Map p106, C3

Carve out a slip on the communal table between the hipsters, or get your own slab of wood on the elegant,

Bodybuilder at Muscle Beach (p105)

tented stone terrace, and dine on delicious and imaginative small plates (think: raw yellowtail spiced with chili and mint and drenched in olive oil and blood orange), and sensational thin-crust, wood-fired pizza. If all you fancy is a gourmet sandwich, salad or a pizza, hit **GTA**, the takeout cafe next door. (📞310-450-1429; www.gjelina. com; 1429 Abbot Kinney Blvd; dishes $8-28; 🕐lunch & dinner; 👶; 🚌 BBB 1)

Joe's
CALIFORNIAN-FRENCH $$$

3 ✂️ Map p106, B2

Like a fine wine, Joe's only gets better with age. It's casual yet stylish, with gimmick-free Cal-French food. The best deal here is the fabulous three-course, prix-fixe lunch for $18. No cell

Top Tip

Walk this Way

Abbot Kinney Blvd is frequently celebrating...something. In late September, the **Abbot Kinney Festival** (www.abbotkinney.org) draws thousands of revelers, as does the now institutionalized **First Friday** (www.abbotkinney1stfridays. com) art walks, when the galleries and shops stay open late and you can roam all night with the tramps, hippies, weirdos, fashionistas, yuppies, hotties and squares.

phones allowed!(☎310-399-5811; www.
joesrestaurant.com; 1023 Abbot Kinney Blvd;
dishes $13-32; ☺noon-2:30pm Tue-Fri, 11am-
2:30pm Sat & Sun, 6-10pm Sun & Tue-Thu,
6-11pm Fri & Sat; 🚇BBB 1)

Axe ASIAN FUSION $$

 4 Map p106, B2

It's good vibes all around at this
minimalist-chic space (pronounced
'a-*shay*') where hip, eco-conscious patrons tuck into sharp-flavored dishes
woven together from whatever is local,
organic and in season. We're partial
to the basic rice bowl with chicken.
(☎310-664-9787; www.axerestaurant.
com; 1009 Abbot Kinney Blvd; dishes $9-22;
☺lunch & dinner Wed-Fri, brunch & dinner Sat
& Sun; P; 🚇BBB 1)

Understand
Art is All Around Us

Who needs galleries when
you've got outdoor art? Just ask
Jonathan Borofsky's 30ft sad-
faced ballerina clown at the corner
of Main St and Rose Ave. Or walk
one block south to ponder Claes
Oldenburg and Coosje van Brug-
gen's massive binoculars, flanking
the Frank Gehry–designed Chiat/
Day building. As for murals, Venice
has a plethora, so be sure to look
up while you walk. Along Ocean
Front Walk, check out Rip Cronk's
Venice Reconstituted and *Hom-
age to a Starry Night,* a tribute to
Vincent Van Gogh.

Abbot's Pizza Co PIZZA $

 5 Map p106, C3

Surfers have savored Abbot's Pizza
gourmet slices for years, but word of
the crisp, bagel-crusted specialties –
tequila-lime chicken, wild mushroom –
has spread beyond the flip-flop crowd
that fills the handful of tables at this
elevator-sized joint. (1407 Abbot Kinney
Blvd; slices from $4; ☺11am-11pm; 🍴👶;
🚇BBB 1)

Seed VEGETARIAN $

 6 Map p106, B3

A new-school macrobiotic veggie joint.
They make sandwiches from roasted
vegetables or Italian soy-sage, rice
bowls with tempeh or seitan, and
their tempeh burgers look dynamite.
They have some indoor seating, but
you're here for the earth lovin' food,
not atmosphere. (www.seedkitchen.com;
1604 Pacific Ave; meals $9-12; ☺lunch &
dinner; 🚇BBB 1)

Mao's Kitchen CHINESE $

 7 Map p106, B3

Cheap and cheerful, Mao's feeds the
local proletariat with country-style
Chinese prepared with So Cal flair
(read: fresh ingredients, no MSG).
Savvy eaters take advantage of the
bargain lunches served until 5pm,
and it's open till the wee hours (3am)
on weekends. (☎310-581-8305; www.
maoskitchen.com; 1512 Pacific Ave; dishes
$5-11; ☺11:30am-10:30pm Sun-Thu, to 3am
Fri & Sat; 🍴👶; 🚇BBB 1)

DAVID PEEVERS/LONELY PLANET IMAGES ©

Mao's Kitchen

Lemonade
MARKET, CAFE **$**

8 Map p106, C4

An imaginative market-cafe with a line-up of tasty salads (think: watermelon radish and chili or tamarind pork and spicy carrots), stockpots bubbling with lamb and stewed figs or miso-braised short ribs, and they have six kinds of lemonade. (www.leomonadela.com; 1661 Abbot Kinney Blvd; meals $8-12; ⊙lunch & dinner; ; BBB1, MTA 33)

Oscar's Cerveteca
MEXICAN FUSION **$$**

9 Map p106, C1

It's an addictive gourmet Mexican kitchen with certain fusion digres-

sions (like the Asian pulled-pork sandwich). The patio is inviting, but so is the stylish interior, what with that wide marble bar, 10 craftsman drafts (this is a *cerveteca,* or beer bar, after all), and global tunes on the sound system. (523 Rose Ave; mains $11-16; ⊙5pm-11pm Mon-Thu, to midnight Fri, 2pm-midnight Sat, to 11pm Sun; BBB 3)

Wurstkuche
SAUSAGE, BEER **$**

10 Map p106, D2

Set in a brick-house loft, but sealed off from the on-rushing madness of Lincoln Blvd, this new German sausage and beer *haus* specializes in three things: gourmet and classic grilled sausages; fine Belgian, German and North American beers; and

Belgian fries with ample dipping sauces. Highly recommended. (www.wurstkuche.com; 625 Lincoln Blvd; dishes $4-8; ⏱11am-midnight, bar to 2am; 🚌BBB 3)

Fig Tree's Café
CALIFORNIA **$$**

11 ✖ Map p106, A1

The best eats on the boardwalk. Here you can munch shiitake omelets made with organic eggs, ginger noodles, and a pesto-brushed, arugula-dressed salmon sandwich, and veg-heads will dig the spinach nut burger. Meals come with complimentary sea views. (www.figtreescafe.com; 429 Ocean Front Walk; mains from $11; ⏱breakfast, lunch & dinner; 🚌BBB 1)

Drinking

Venice Beach Wines
WINE BAR

A sweet and cozy hideaway with louvered benches and tables close together, at Venice Beach Wines, near Oscar's Cerveteca (see 9 ✖ Map p106, C1), you will commune with strangers as you sip international wines by the glass or bottle (including a complex and invigorating French Syrah) and munch charcuterie, *pizzettas* and the like. For dessert try the *pot de crème*. It's 75% cacao and 100% orgasmic. (www.venicebeachwines.com; 529 Rose Ave; ⏱11:30am-11pm Mon-Thu, to midnight Fri, 9am-midnight Sat, to 11pm Sun; 🚌BBB 3)

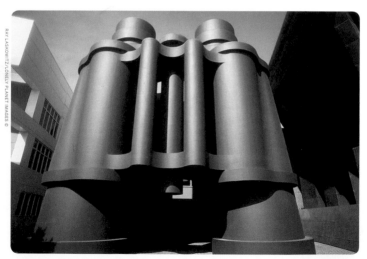

RAY LASKOWITZ/LONELY PLANET IMAGES ©

Binocular sculpture designed by Claes Oldenburg and Coosje van Bruggen (see the boxed text, p108)

Abbot's Pizza Co (p108)

Hal's Bar & Grill BAR

12 📍 Map p106, C3

The name may evoke brass and wood, but Hal's dining room is an industrial loft brightened by revolving art from local artists who treat the place like an extended living room. They have free live jazz on Sunday and Monday. (📞310-396-3105; www.halsbarandgrill.com; 1349 Abbot Kinney Blvd; 🚌BBB 1, MTA 33)

Brig BAR

13 📍 Map p106, C4

Old-timers remember this place as a divey pool hall owned by ex-boxer Babe Brandelli (that's him and his wife on the outside mural). Now it's a bit sleeker, and attracts a trendy mix

of grown-up beach bums, arty professionals and artists. (www.thebrig.com; 1515 Abbot Kinney Blvd; 🅿; 🚌BBB 1, MTA 33)

Intelligentsia CAFE

If you are the sort who prefers clean lines and laboratory-like order to unwashed coffee-house clutter, who enjoys being dressed down by meansexy Ivy League baristas, if you thirst for Joe prepared with egotistic aplomb and the Zen of pure love, then wait in line at Intelligentsia, located near Hal's Bar & Grill (see 12 📍 Map p106, C3), with the salt-and-pepper protohipsters, pay your $5 and enjoy. (www.intelligentsiacoffee.com; 1331 Abbot Kinney Blvd; ⏰6am-8pm Sun-Wed, to 11pm Thu-Sat; 🚌BBB 1, MTA 33)

Shopping

A + R Store
GIFTS

14 Map p106, B3

This is top-end industrial design and a great browse, with interesting ceramic speakers, ergonomic headphones, chairs and scissors (!), wooden toys and strange-yet-alluring high-format cameras. (☎800-913-0071; www.aplusrstore.com; 1121 Abbot Kinney Blvd; ☺closed Mon; ☑BBB 1)

Alternative
CLOTHING

Alternative, close to Hal's Bar & Grill (see **12** ☺ Map p106, C3), built its name on organic cotton and recycled poly hoodies and tees, but has expanded its collection to include beachy, hip flannels, cardigans, skirts and slacks. Who cares if they have man purses? You don't *have* to buy one. (www.alternativeapparel. com; 1337 Abbot Kinney Blvd; ☑BBB 1, MTA 33)

Gebert Gallery
GALLERY

A glass-and-concrete modern-art light box, and we think the best art gallery in Venice. The paintings here at Gebert Gallery, near Hal's Bar & Grill (see **12** ☺ Map p106, C3), are always top-shelf and from known artists. Highly recommended. (☎310-450-9897; www. gebertgallery.com; 1345 Abbot Kinney Blvd; ☑BBB 1, MTA 33)

Altered Space
GALLERY

15 Map p106, C3

One of our favorite Abbot Kinney galleries, with rotating exhibits in the upper tier (we glimpsed a cool pipe sculpture collection and groovy driftwood sculptures) and vintage jewelry cases suspended in the downstairs space. (www.alteredspacegallery.com; 1221 Abbot Kinney Blvd; ☑BBB 1, MTA 33)

Bazaar
GIFTS

16 Map p106, B3

One of several fun and funky vintage clothing and antique galleries on Abbot Kinney. In addition to some fabulous vintage silver, we glimpsed a gorgeous 19th-century indigo farmer's frock from France. It was going for just $1400! The point is it's a fun place to treasure hunt. (1108c Abbot Kinney Blvd; ☑MA 33, 333)

Heist
CLOTHING

17 Map p106, B3

A new boutique and one of the more 'affordable' shops on Abbot Kinney. The collection ventures a little deeper into Venice's hippie roots, but is still quite elegant. Think Anthropologie, but indie. (www.shopheist.com; 1100 Abbot Kinney; ☑BBB 1)

Strange Invisible Perfumes
PERFUMES, LOTIONS

18 Map p106, B3

Walk-ins welcome at this upscale but accessible perfumery where fragrances are crafted from all-natural essential oils. Discover that perfect soulful scent at the consultation bar or wander past cool, lavender-toned walls for an equally fascinating array of naturally fragranced cleansers, scrubs and creams. (☎310-314-1505; www.siperfumes.com; 1138 Abbot Kinney Blvd; 🚇BBB 1)

Surfing Cowboys FURNITURE

19 🔒 Map p106, C4

Giddy up, bro. Bring your lasso and your wallet to the funkiest purveyor of midcentury furniture and surf memorabilia this side of, well, anywhere. Surfing Cowboys is filled with vintage surfboards and skateboards, retro but comfy couches, historic beach photos and gently worn cowboy boots. (www.surfingcowboys.com; 1624 Abbot Kinney Blvd; 🕒closed Mon; 🚇BBB 1, MTA 33)

Warakuku SHOES, FASHION

Warakuku, close to Altered Space (see**15** 🔒 Map p106, C3), is a compact Japanese-owned shop for shoe lovers. It blends Far East couture with mainstream street brands such as Puma and Converse. Some 60% of the shoes are imported from Japan, the rest are domestic limited editions, and the prices are damned reasonable. (www.warakukuusa.com; 1225 Abbot Kinney Blvd; 🚇BBB 1, MTA 33)

Entrance to Strange Invisible Perfumes

Civilianaire DENIM

A new brand from the brains behind Lucky Brand, the high-end line Civilianaire, near Surfing Cowboys (see**19** 🔒 Map p106, C4), is influenced by utilitarian and, yes, military garb, not that anyone who ever buys it will put in a day of blue-collar hustle and sweat. (www.civilianaire.com; 1522 1/2 Abbot Kinney Blvd; 🕒11am-8pm Mon-Sat, to 7pm Sun; 🚇BBB 1, MTA 33)

Local Life
Manhattan Beach

A bastion of surf music and the birthplace of beach volleyball, Manhattan Beach may have gone chic, but that salty-dog heart still beats. Yes, the downtown area along Manhattan Beach Blvd has seen an explosion of trendy restaurants and boutiques, but the real action is beachside, where the bikinis are small, the waves kind and the smiles are as oversized as those sunglasses.

Getting There

🚗 **Car** Two exits of I-405 serve Manhattan Beach, including Rosecrans Blvd and Inglewood Ave, which merges with Manhattan Beach Blvd.

🚌 **Bus** MTA 126

❶ Sand Dune Park

The recently renovated **Sand Dune Park** (www.ci.manhattan-beach.ca.us; cnr 33rd & Bell Ave; ⏱7:30am-9pm Apr-Oct, 6am-8pm Nov-Mar; Ⓟ🚻) requires reservations if you wish to access the long, deep 100ft-high natural sand dune. Your kids will love hurling themselves down the dune again and again.

❷ Uncle Bill's Pancake House

Sexy surfers, tottering toddlers and gabbing girlfriends – everybody comes to **Uncle Bill's** (☎310-545-5177; 1305 N Highland Ave; ⏱6am-3pm Mon-Fri, 7am-3pm Sat & Sun; 🖊🚻) for the famous pancakes and big fat omelets (try the 'Istanbul' made with turkey).

❸ Wright's

Easily the grooviest boutique in Manhattan Beach. **Wright's** (☎310-376-8553; www.wrightsclothing.com; 232 Manhattan Beach Blvd) traffics in beach-chic gear.

❹ Elleni

Because originality will get you everywhere, and there are no two more severe addictions suffered by LA woman than shoes and chocolate, that's all they've got at **Elleni** (☎310-376-3553; www.ellenicoutoure.com; 1100 Manhattan Ave).

❺ Ercole's

A funky counterpoint to the HD-inundated, design-heavy sports bars on Manhattan Beach Blvd. **Ercole's** (☎310-372-1997; 1101 Manhattan Ave; ⏱10am-2am) is a dark, chipped, well-irrigated hole with a barn door open to everyone from salty barflies to yuppie pub crawlers to volleyball stars and wobbly coeds – since 1927.

❻ Roundhouse Aquarium

Family fun awaits at the compact **Roundhouse Marine Studies Lab & Aquarium** (www.roundhouseaquarium.org; suggested donation $2; ⏱3pm-sunset Mon-Fri, 10am-sunset Sat & Sun; 🚻) at the end of the 928ft-long pier. Pat a slimy sea cucumber, see Nemo the clownfish up close, and check out the new deep-ocean tank.

❼ Mama D's

This neighborhood Italian joint fits like a well-worn shoe. **Mama D's** (☎310-456-1492; 1125 Manhattan Ave; ⏱lunch & dinner; 🚻) thin-crust pizzas, homemade ravioli, tangy cioppino and freshly baked bread, all served with a smile, keep regulars coming back for more.

❽ MB Post

The best new kitchen in the South Bay, trendy but friendly and unvarnished **MB Post** (☎310-545-5405; www.eatmbpost.com; 1142 Manhattan Ave; ⏱lunch & dinner; 🚻) offers globally inspired tapas. Walk in and dine at the long communal tables in the bar, or make a reservation and get cozy at a small table in the dining room.

Local Life
Long Beach

Long Beach has come
a long way since its
working-class oil and navy
days. Over the past dec-
ade, LA's southernmost
seaside town has quietly
reinvented its gritty
downtown and, recession-
related vacancies notwith-
standing, made itself an
attractive place to live and
party. Most of the action's
along the waterfront,
on Pine Ave or in nearby
Belmont Shore.

Getting There

Ⓜ **Metro** Metro Rail Blue
Line is the stress-free way
to get to Long Beach.

🚌 **Bus** Once downtown
you can walk or catch the
red Passport buses, which
swing by the points of inter-
est (free within downtown,
or $1.25).

❶ Queen Mary

Long Beach's 'flagship' attraction, the **Queen Mary** (www.queenmary.com; 1126 Queens Hwy; adult/senior/child $25/22/12; ⏰10am-6pm; Ⓟ) is a grand and supposedly haunted British prewar luxury liner. Study the photos and memorabilia and you may be able to envision dapper gents escorting ladies in heels and gowns to the art deco lounge for cocktails or the sumptuous Grand Salon for dinner.

❷ Aquarium of the Pacific

The **Aquarium of the Pacific** (www.aquariumofpacific.org; 100 Aquarium Way; adult/child/senior $25/13/22; ⏰9am-6pm; Ⓟ 👫) is a vast, high-tech indoor ocean where sharks dart, jellyfish dance and sea lions frolic. More than 12,000 creatures inhabit four re-created habitats. Parking costs $8.

❸ Museum of Latin American Art

This gem presents a rare survey of Latin American art created since 1945. Cecilia Míguez' whimsical bronze statuettes, Eduardo Kingman's wrenching portraits of indigenous people and Arnaldo Roche Rabel's intensely spiritual abstracts are among the many outstanding pieces in the permanent collection of the **Museum of Latin American Art** (www.molaa.org; 628 Alamitos Ave; adult/student & senior/child under 12yr $9/6/free; ⏰11am-5pm Wed, Fri-Sun, to 9pm Thu; Ⓟ).

❹ Basement Lounge

Like the name says, **Basement Lounge** (www.basementloungelb.com; 149 Linden Ave; ⏰from 6pm) is set beneath a historic, arched-brick edifice in the East Village Arts District. LB's best DJs spin here.

Further Afield
Belmont Shore

If downtown Long Beach feels urban and corporate, **Belmont Shore** (E 2nd St btwn Linvingston Dr & Bay Shore Ave; 🚃 red Passport) exudes quintessential SoCal laid-backness. It has a fine beach with a pier for fishing and sunsets, and keeps it real along a buzzy four-block-long strip of mostly indie boutiques and cafes.

Claire's at the Museum

Set in a hundred-year-old Craftsman masterpiece, **Claire's** (www.lbma.org/cafe.html; 2300 Ocean Ave; ⏰11am-8pm Thu, to 3pm Fri, 8am-3pm Sat & Sun; Ⓟ) serves tasty California cooking with exquisite views.

Long Beach Museum of Art

The beachfront location is breathtaking, and the permanent collection of the **Long Beach Museum of Art** (www.lbma.org; 2300 E Ocean Blvd; adult/student & senior/child under 12 $7/6/free; free on Friday; ⏰11am-8pm Thu, to 5pm Fri-Sun) boasts midcentury pieces and contemporary work by regional artists.

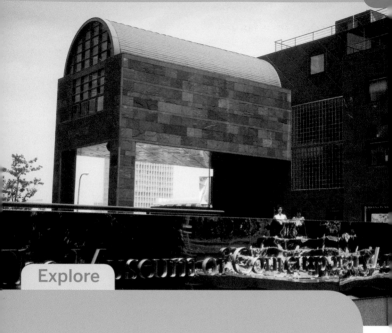

Explore

Downtown

Downtown Los Angeles has gone from derelict to fascinating in a decade. Here's stunning architecture from 19th-century beaux arts to futuristic Frank Gehry, world-class music, top-notch art, superb dining and sinful cocktails. It's a power nexus and a gritty hipster haven for indie artists and designers. Don't expect Manhattan, but momentum is undeniably here, and now's the time to explore.

The Sights in a Day

☀ Have breakfast at the **$.05 Diner** (p129) before meandering down Broadway past the old theaters to the **Fashion District** (p122), where even if there isn't a sample sale on you can explore the **California Market Center** (p123), absorb the general fashionistas vibe, and rummage through **Virgo** (p133) and **Santee Alley** (p123). Hit the epic **Grammy Museum** (p126) before heading north.

☀ Grab lunch among suits, designers and artists at **Bottega Louie** (p128) before strolling north past Pershing Square and into the Financial District. From here it's an easy walk two blocks north to the **Walt Disney Concert Hall** (p120), where you can catch the last tour of the day. Then walk southeast to the **Museum of Contemporary Art** (pictured left; p126) and the **Grand Central Market** (p126).

☾ If it's a summer Friday night, you can start your evening with free live music at the **California Plaza** (p128). Otherwise, head up to the **Standard Rooftop Bar** (p131) for a sundowner, then stroll into Little Tokyo where you can visit the **MOCA Geffen Contemporary** (p126) before ducking into the **Lazy Ox Canteen** (p129) or the **Spice Table** (p128) for gourmet fusion. Afterward, wander back down to the **Association** (p130) or **Las Perlas** (p130), or both, for a nightcap.

 Top Sights

Walt Disney Concert Hall (p120)

○ **Local Life**

Shopping the Fashion District (p122)

♥ **Best of Los Angeles**

Eating

Bottega Louie (p128)

Philippe the Original (p129)

Drinking

Las Perlas (p130)

Association (p130)

Sights

Grand Central Market (p126)

Grammy Museum (p126)

Museum of Contemporary Art (MOCA; p126)

Getting There

Ⓜ **Metro** Downtown is well connected to Hollywood by the Metro Red Line, while Metrolink connects downtown with Long Beach and Burbank.

🚌 **Bus** MTA, LA's principal transit authority, connects downtown with all other parts of town. Santa Monica's Big Blue Bus connects downtown with the shore.

Top Sights
Walt Disney Concert Hall

A molten blend of steel, music and psychedelic architecture, Frank Gehry pulled out all the stops for his iconic concert venue that's the home base of the Los Angeles Philharmonic, but also hosts contemporary bands such as Phoenix and classic jazz men such as Sonny Rollins. The building is a gravity-defying sculpture of heaving and billowing stainless-steel walls that conjure visions of a ship adrift in a rough sea.

◉ Map p124, E2

☎ 213-972-7211

111 S Grand Ave

tours free, shows vary

⏱ tours 10am-2pm most days

Ⓜ Civic Center, ⬛14/37, 55/355, 60, 439

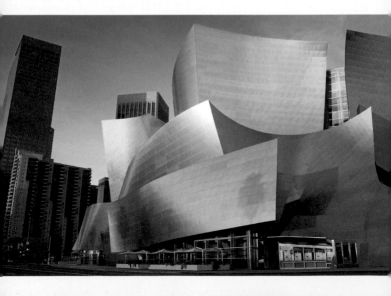

Don't Miss

Los Angeles Philharmonic

The only way to experience the auditorium is to buy tickets. The **Los Angeles Philharmonic** (www. laphil.com) curates the calendar and, in addition to classical shows, it often hosts jazz luminaries. The room feels like the inside of a finely crafted cello, clad in walls of smooth Douglas fir. Even seats below the giant pipe organ offer excellent sight lines.

Red Cat

The curious **Red Cat** (www.redcat.org; 631 W 2nd St) name is an acronym for Roy and Edna Disney/ Cal Arts Theater. Downtown's most avante garde theater and art gallery has its own address (and auditorium) in the Walt Disney Concert Hall complex. Admission to the gallery, which rotates art exhibitions every six weeks, is free.

Pipe Organ

The stunning pipe organ, a gift to LA county from the Toyota Corporation, incorporates 6134 pipes and took over 2000 hours to tune. The longest pipe is over 32ft long and weighs upwards of 800 pounds. Shipped by sea from Germany, the instrument's total weight is over 40 metric tons. And it sounds just that big.

☑ Top Tips

▶ Self-guided tours narrated by John Lithgow are offered most days, but 60-minute docent-led tours may also be available. Consult the schedule online.

▶ To save money on parking, find a cheaper lot in Little Tokyo or the Jewelry District and walk.

▶ Tours do not include a glimpse of the auditorium, so the best way to experience the concert hall is to buy tickets and see a show.

✕ Take a Break

Little Tokyo is about six blocks away. If you're hungry for fusion, hit the Spice Table (p128), or get gritty and grab an epic ramen bowl at Daikokuya (p129). Or stay glamorous and head to the Standard Rooftop Bar (p131) for a drink before or after a show.

Local Life
Shopping the Fashion District

Bargain hunters love this frantic 100-block warren of fashion. Deals can be amazing, but first-timers are often bewildered by the district's size and immense selection. And by the sheer juxtaposition of sassy fashionistas in minis, knee-high boots and new-school cardigans wandering among drunks with neck tattoos and a perma-haze.

❶ Back to School

Technically, it's a bit west of the district, but the **Fashion Institute of Design and Merchandising** (FIDM; www.fidm.edu; 919 S Grand Ave; ⏱10am-4pm Tue-Sat; 🚇MTA 14/37), a private college with an international student body, is very much part of its soul. The gallery has some interesting rotating exhibits, including costumes worn in Academy Award–nominated movies.

2 Sample Sales

Every last Friday of the month from 9am to 2pm, clued-in fashionistas descend upon the corner of 9th and Olympic armed with cash and attitude to catfight it out for designer clothes priced below wholesale. Their destinations: the showrooms at the **Gerry Building** (www.gerrybuilding.com; 910 S Los Angeles St; 🚇MTA 66), the **Cooper** (www.cooperdesignspace.com; 860 S Los Angeles St; 🚇MTA 66) and the **New Mart** (www.newmart.net/samplesales.htm; 127 E 9th St; 🚇MTA 66).

3 Bargain District

One of the most laid-back and festive corners of the district, there are over 150 shops and stalls crammed into this single laneway. **Santee Alley** (www.thesanteealley.com; Santee St & 12th St; ⏱9:30am-6pm; 🚇MTA 66) is known for its designer knockoffs.

4 Quick Fix

Need that quick fix to sate you through the sample-sale madness? Head to the **Market** (www.marketrestaurants.com; 862 S Los Angeles St; mains $8.50-11; ⏱lunch Mon-Fri; ✈🚻; 🚇MTA 66) for a pressed Cuban (citrus-glazed pork, ham and manchego) or a seared-ahi and soba-noodle salad. Eat at common, brushed-metal tables with fellow shoppers and steely-eyed designers.

5 The Hub

Although it's no longer the hippest building in the district, the **California Market Center** (www.californiamarketcenter.com; 110 E 9th St; 🚇MTA 66) remains its axis, and resident designers hold sample sales here.

6 Posh Hour

Set on the whimsical ground floor of the New Mart is **Tiara Café** (www.tiara-cafe-la.com; 127 E 9th St; mains $9-18; ⏱lunch Mon-Fri; ✈🚻; 🚇MTA 66), with pink walls, soaring ceilings and thick granite columns. The tables are packed with fashionistas and the food is fantastic.

7 Cocktails

The newest Fashion District well, **Pattern Bar** (www.patternbar.com; 100 W 9th St; ⏱noon-midnight Sun-Thu, to 2am Fri, 6pm-2am Sat; 🚇MTA 66) comes with pebbled marble floors, vintage bar stools and a classic rock soundtrack. Cocktails are christened for fashion icons like DVF and McQueen, and it serves tapas and *arepas*.

8 Art for the People

A massive, mad swirl of art lovers invades downtown once a month for free, self-guided, liberally lubricated **Downtown Art Walks** (www.downtownartwalk.org; ⏱noon-9pm 2nd Thu of the month) that link more than 40 galleries and museums across the downtown grid. You'll find most between 3rd and 9th and Broadway and Main.

A

B

C

D

1

Chick Hearn Ct

Georgia St

Pasadena Fwy

Staples
Center

Cottage Pl

Francisco St

28 ✪

2 ◉ Grammy
Museum

S Figueroa St

2

W 12th St

S Hope St

S Flower St

7th
St/Metro
Center

ARCO
Plaza

**SOUTH
PARK**

Macy's
Plaza

W 7th St

23 ◉ Maguire Gardens

Bank of
America
Plaza

Grand
Hope Park

Ⓜ

ℹ

S Hope St

W 11th St

S Grand Ave

Richard Riordan
Central Library

S Olive St

W Olympic Blvd

9th St

8th St

8 ⊗

16 ⊗

S Grand Ave

Midway Pl

W 9th St

21 ◉

**FINANCIAL
DISTRICT**

California
Plaza

◉**7**

S Hill St

**JEWELRY
DISTRICT**

◉**32**

Pershing
Square

Ⓜ Pershing
Square

S Broadway

✪26

W 6th St

25 ✪

◉**1**

3

S Main St

✪ **30**

S Broadway

W 5th St

W 4th St

◉
Grand
Central
Market

S Los Angeles St

22 California
Market
Center

33
◉

9 ⊗

◉**34**

◉

Santee St

◉

S Spring St

27 ✪

31 ◉

**FASHION
DISTRICT**

36

Harlem Pl

Harlem Pl

E Olympic Blvd

◉

19

15

35 **13**

◉

◉

⊗

Maple Ave

E 11th St

E 9th St

18
◉

**LITTLE
TOKYO**

Wall St

Flower
Market

E 8th St

E 7th St

E 6th St

E 5th St

Winston St

E 4th St

E 3rd St

4

San Julian St

S San Pedro St

San Julian St

5

Agatha St

Crocker St

Towne Ave

Stanford Ave

ARTS DISTRICT Ⓟ

For reviews see	
◉ Top Sights	p120
◉ Sights	p126
⊗ Eating	p128
◉ Drinking	p130
✪ Entertainment	p131
◉ Shopping	p133

E

F

G

H

1

2

3

4

5

N Beaydry Ave

Beverly Blvd

W Temple St

College St

Pasadena Fwy

W 3rd St

W 1st St

N Figueroa St

Santa Ana Fwy

W Cesar E Chavez Ave

S Hope St

Walt Disney Concert Hall

29

Alpine St

Alpine Park

3 **Museum of Contemporary Art (MOCA)**

S Olive St

N Grand Ave

Civic Center

6 **Cathedral of Our Lady of the Angels**

Yale St

W College St

Civic Center/ Tom Bradley

W Temple St

CHINATOWN

Grand Central Market

N Broadway

Arcadia St

N Hill St

N Broadway

Chinatown

N Spring St

Ord St

N Spring St

N Alameda St

24

N Main St

12

N Main St

E 2nd St

N Los Angeles St

El Pueblo de Los Angeles

5 **Pueblo de Los Angeles**

14

4 **Union Station**

Judge John Aiso St

17

Amtrak

Japanese Village Plaza

Union Station/ Gateway Transit Center

James Irvine Garden

N Alameda St

10

Metrolink Station

N Vignes St

E Cesar E Chavez Ave

11

E 1st St

E Temple St

Banning St

N Vignes St

Santa Ana Fwy

20

Sights

Grand Central Market

MARKET

1 Map p124, D3

Here on the ground floor of a 1905 beaux-arts building, where architect Frank Lloyd Wright once kept an office, you can stroll along the sawdust-sprinkled aisles beneath old-timey ceiling fans and neon signs, past stalls piled high with produce, and plenty of lunch counters for snacking on ceviche, shawarma or chicken soup. (www.grandcentralmarket.com; 317 S Broadway; ⊙9am-6pm; 🚌MTA 745, 10/48)

Understand

Broadway Theater District

Until eclipsed by Hollywood in the mid-1920s, Broadway was LA's entertainment hub with no fewer than a dozen theaters built in a riot of styles, from beaux arts to East Indian to Spanish Gothic. Their architectural and historic significance even earned them a spot on the National Register of Historic Places. However, since this area is now a decidedly ungentrified slice of cut-rate retail and gritty urban action, they're usually closed to the public. The best way to see them is by joining one of the excellent tours offered by the **LA Conservancy** (www.laconservancy.org).

Grammy Museum

MUSEUM

2 Map p124, A1

Get lost in interactive exhibits, which define, differentiate and link musical genres. Glimpse Lester Young's tenor, Yo Yo Ma's cello and Michael's glove. Sound chambers allow you and your friends to remix, sing and rap. (www.grammymuseum.org; 800 W Olympic Blvd; adult/senior/student $12.95/11.95/10.95; ⊙11:30am-7:30pm Mon-Fri, 10am-7:30pm Sat & Sun; Ⓜ Silver Line, 🚌MTA 28)

Museum of Contemporary Art (MOCA)

MUSEUM

3 Map p124, E2

Architect Arata Isozaki built this conglomeration of cubes, pyramids and cylinders to house renowned collections of abstract expressionism, pop art, minimalism and photography from the 5000-piece permanent collection. Same-day tickets are valid at Little Tokyo's MOCA Geffen Contemporary (152 N Central Ave). (📞213-626-6222; www.moca.org; 250 S Grand Ave; adult/student & senior $10/5, free 5-8pm Thu; ⊙11am-5pm Mon & Fri, to 8pm Thu, to 6pm Sat & Sun; Ⓜ Silver Line)

Union Station

LANDMARK

4 Map p124, G4

Built on the site of LA's original Chinatown, it opened in 1939 as America's last grand rail station. It's a glamorous exercise in Mission Revival with art deco accents. The marble-floored main hall, with cathedral ceilings, original leather chairs and grand

Waiting room at Union Station

chandeliers, is breathtaking. (800 N Alameda St; **M**Union Station)

Pueblo de Los Angeles MONUMENT

 5 Map p124, G4

LA was a full-blown community a good 100 years before DW Griffith showed up. Grab a map at restored Firehouse No 1 (the Plaza Firehouse) then wander through narrow Olvera St's vibrant Mexican-themed stalls. For LA's oldest building, see **Avila Adobe** (213-628-1274; Olvera St; 9am-4pm) then walk through the **Sepulveda House** (213-628-1274; 622 N Main St; 9am-4pm Mon-Fri, 10am-3pm Sat & Sun) and its visitor center to see a restored 1800s-era kitchen and bedroom. (213-628-1274; www.lacity.org/elp; btwn Main & Alameda Sts; admission free; tour office 10am-3pm; **M**Union Station)

Cathedral of Our Lady of the Angels CHURCH

6 Map p124, F3

Architect Jose Rafael Moneo rewrote the cathedral builders' rulebook in 2002 with this flowing, free-form church complete with plazas, colonnades and a distinct disregard for right angles. His incorporation of regional styles and historic influences provides a welcoming air. (213-680-5200; www.olacathedral.org; 555 W Temple St; admission free; 6:30am-6pm Mon-Fri, 9am-6pm Sat, 7am-6pm Sun; **M**Civic Center)

DAVID PEEVERS/LONELY PLANET IMAGES ©

Grand Central Market (p126)

California Plaza LANDMARK

 7 Map p124, D2

California Plaza hosts Grand Performances (www.grandperformances.org), one of the best free summer performance series. (350 S Grand Ave; MPershing Square)

Eating

Bottega Louie ITALIAN $$

8 Map p124, C2

The upscale Tuscan market cuisine and marbled grace lures the artsy loft set and white-collar worker bees alike. The open-kitchen crew – all in chef's whites – carves deli meats and slices cheese, steams shellfish in white wine and crafts wood-fire thin-crust pies. (213-802-1470; www.bottegalouie.com; 700 S Grand Ave; mains $12-20; breakfast, lunch & dinner; M7th St/Metro Center)

Gorbals EASTERN EUROPEAN FUSION $$

9 Map p124, C3

An Eastern European tapas joint set in the old Alexandria Hotel lobby. Menu mainstays include sublime bacon-wrapped matzos balls served with pink-hot horseradish mayo, and latkes with smoked applesauce. (213-488-3408; www.thegorbalsla.com; 501 S Spring St; dishes $6-17; 6pm-midnight Mon-Wed, to 2am Thu-Sat; MPershing Square)

Spice Table SOUTHEAST ASIAN FUSION $$

10 Map p124, E5

The latest hot spot to hit the Little Tokyo streets, set in a super cool, minimalist, brick-house loft, serving spicy dishes culled from Southeast Asia. There are satays, noodle and rice dishes, chicken curry, beef rendang and spicy sandwiches at lunch. (213-620-1840; www.thespicetable.com; 114 S Central Ave; mains $7.50-13; lunch & dinner Mon-Sat; MLittle Tokyo)

Sushi Gen JAPANESE $$

11 Map p124, E5

When you ask Little Tokyo locals where to eat the freshest and tastiest sushi, they will point to this blink-and-you'll-miss-it spot in the Honda Plaza mini-mall. And if you see them again, you will thank them profusely. (213-617-0552; 422 E 2nd St; sushi &

sashimi $6-30; ☺lunch & dinner Mon-Sat; Ⓜ Little Tokyo)

Philippe the Original

DINER $

12 Map p124, G3

From beat cops to stressed-out attorneys to smooching couples, everyone loves Philippe's, where the French-dip sandwich was invented a century ago. Order a crusty roll filled with meat (we go with the lamb 'double-dipped'), and hunker down at communal tables on the sawdust-covered floor. Cash only. (www.philippes.com; sandwiches $6-7.50; 1001 N Alameda St; ☺breakfast, lunch & dinner; Ⓟ ♿; 🚌MTA 76)

Blossom

VIETNAMESE $

13 Map p124, D3

This stylish kitchen churns out fresh and tasty Vietnamese food on the cheap. Start with the *goi cuon* (shrimp and pork spring rolls), and follow it with some spicy *pho* (noodle soup) paired with a bottle of French burgundy ($25). (www.blossomrestaurant.com; 426 S Main St; mains $8-11; ☺lunch & dinner Mon-Sat; Ⓜ Pershing Square)

Lazy Ox Canteen

PUB $$

14 Map p124, E4

Fusion tapas in cedar-paneled environs. Think pig's ear *chicharon*, seared albacore with pickled apples, lentils and bacon, and crispy clams. Pair them with something from the creative beer and wine list. (📞213-626-5299; www.lazyoxcanteen.com; 241 S San

Pedro; dishes $5-18; ☺lunch & dinner; ♿; Ⓜ Little Tokyo)

$.05 Diner

DINER $

15 Map p124, C3

Named for the intersection of 5th and Main Sts, and termed 'the Nickel' by nearby skid-row residents, this kitschy red-vinyl joint reimagines American-diner fare. Avocados are stuffed with quinoa salad, burgers are piled with poblano chilis, and don't sleep on the maple-glazed bacon donut. (www.5cdiner.com; 524 S Main St; mains $8.50-11.75; ☺breakfast & lunch Tue-Sun, dinner Tue-Sat; Ⓜ Pershing Square)

Mas Malo

MEXICAN $$

16 Map p124, C2

A tasty extension of Robert Luna's Silver Lake brand set in a marvelous historic bank building beneath the erstwhile 7 Grand. Enjoy enchiladas stuffed with bacon-wrapped prawns, a Caesar salad spiced with jalapeño or snapper sautéed in habanero white-wine garlic butter. (📞213-985-4332; www.masmalorestaurant.com; 515 W 7th St; mains $10-16; ☺lunch & dinner; Ⓜ7th St/Metro Center)

Daikokuya

JAPANESE $

17 Map p124, E4

If you are partial to ramen, fall into this funky Little Tokyo diner that leaves the hungry people lining the sidewalk and salivating at the prospect of LA's best-loved noodle soup.

RICHARD CUMMINS/LONELY PLANET IMAGES ©

Mexican-themed clothing store at Pueblo de Los Angeles (p127)

(www.daikoku-ten.com; 327 E 1st St; mains $7-13.50; ⏰lunch & dinner; P; MLittle Tokyo)

Drinking

Las Perlas
BAR

18 📍 Map p124, C4

With a hint of Old Mexico whimsy, a chalkboard menu of over 80 tequilas and mezcals, and friendly barkeeps who mix things like egg whites, blackberries and port syrup into new-school takes on the classic margarita, there's a reason (or make that 80 reasons) why we love downtown's best tequila bar. (www.lasperlas.la; 103 E 6th St; ⏰7pm-2am Mon-Sat; 🚌MTA 720)

Association
BAR, LOUNGE

19 📍 Map p124, C3

This hip basement bar flashes old-school glamour with leather bar stools and lounges tucked into intimate coves. But the bar is the thing. We're talking about dozens of whiskeys, ryes, rums and tequilas. The engaging bartenders muddle and mix like pros. Just don't call them 'mixologists.' They hate that. (www.theassociation-la.com; 110 E 6th St; ⏰5pm-2am Mon-Fri, 7pm-2am Sat & Sun; 🚌MTA 720)

One-Eyed Gypsy
BAR

20 📍 Map p124, F5

Set just off the Little Tokyo swirl, this oh-so-dark carnival-themed joint comes with 10 craftsman beers on tap, peaked Arabic arches, a ski-ball arcade-game concession, a stage blessed with a circus curtain and live music nightly. Oh, and it serves a deep-fried Chocodile. Hence the hipster following. (www.one-eyedgypsy.com; 901 E 1st St; ⏱6pm-2am Wed-Sat; Ⓜ Little Tokyo)

Seven Grand
BAR

21 Map p124, C2

A fantastic whiskey bar with tongue-in-cheek hunting decor. There are 175 varieties of amber to explore, rotating DJs and a smoking patio. (www.sevengrand.la; 515 W 7th St; ⏱5pm-2am Mon-Wed, 4pm-2am Thu & Fri, 7pm-2am Sat & Sun; Ⓜ 7th St/Metro Center)

Pattern Bar
BAR

22 Map p124, B3

The newest Fashion District well comes with pebbled marble floors, vintage bar stools, booths and a classic rock soundtrack. It belongs in a film or fashion shoot. Cocktails are christened for fashion icons such as DVF and McQueen and it serves tapas and *arepas*. (www.patternbar.com; 100 W 9th St; ⏱noon-midnight Sun-Thu, to 2am Fri, 6pm-2am Sat; ▯MTA 66)

Standard Rooftop Bar
BAR

23 Map p124, C2

Once you find your way to this rooftop oasis – try escalator, elevator, stairs – the panoramic payoff is immense, with stunning views of skyscrapers backdropped by glowing mountains. On weekends arrive before 7pm to beat the cover and the velvet rope. (☎213-892-8080; www.standardhotels.com; 550 S Flower St; admission after 7pm Fri & Sat $20; ⏱noon-1:30am; Ⓜ 7th St/Metro Center)

Entertainment

Edison
CLUB

24 Map p124, E3

A staircase descends from the ground floor to a steam-punk warren of lounges decorated with Victorian flair and the occasional industrial turbine (remnants from the Edison's days as a private power plant), and is populated by an inviting mix of suits and hipsters. There is a dress code. (☎213-613-0000; www.edisondowntown.com; Harlem Place Alley off 108 W 2nd St; Ⓜ Civic Center)

La Cita
CLUB

25 Map p124, D3

The perfect setting for a midnight afternoon or a wild soul-infused dance party, this red-vinyl Mexican dive bar alternates between a dance club for downtown hipsters – when DJs whip the crowd into a frenzy – and a brassy salsa party featuring top-shelf live acts. Um, no dress code here. (www.lacitabar.com; 336 S Hill St; ⏱10am-2am; Ⓜ Pershing Square)

Q Local Life
How's About a Little Round Ball?

Staples Center (Map p124, A1; www.staplescenter.com; 1111 S Figueroa St; Pico), aka the House that Shaq Built (and then bequeathed to one, Kobe 'Black Mamba' Bryant), is the vortex of pro basketball in LA. It is here that the **Los Angeles Lakers** (www.nba.com/lakers) reign, where the ubiquitous Jack cheers from his floor seats and the **Los Angeles Clippers** (www.nba.com/clippers) suffer in their shadow.

Club Mayan
CLUB, CONCERT VENUE

26 ⭐ Map p124, A3

Kick up your heels during Saturday's Tropical Nights, when a salsa band turns the heat up. Don't know how? Come early for lessons, and note that there is a dress code. On Fridays it's house and hip hop, and it also hosts its share of wrestling events and indie bands with a following. (www.clubmayan.com; 1038 S Hill St; ☺9pm-3am Fri & Sat, varies Sun-Thu; **P**; 🚌MTA 2/302, 728)

Los Angeles Theater Center
THEATER

27 ⭐ Map p124, C3

Housed in the Old Pacific Stock Exchange, which was built in 1915, the downstairs gallery rotates exhibitions curated by the Latino Museum of Art, while the excellent stage shows, produced by the 23-year-old Latino Theater Company, explore culturally diverse material and often feature emerging playwrights. (www.thelatc.org; 514 S Spring St; admission $5-20; ☺gallery noon-6pm Tue-Sat; **M**Pershing Square)

Nokia Theater
CONCERT VENUE

28 ⭐ Map p124, A1

A 7100-seat theater, which was christened by the Eagles and the Dixie Chicks when it opened in 2007, has hosted Neil Young, Anita Baker and Ricky Gervais. Check the website for info on upcoming shows. (www.nokiatheatrelive.com; 777 Chick Hearn Court; ticket prices vary; **M**Silver Line, 🚌MTA 81, 728)

Music Center of LA County
PERFORMING ARTS

29 ⭐ Map p124, E2

At this linchpin of the downtown performing arts scene, splashy musicals and Placido Domingo–helmed operas play to capacity at the Ahmanson Theatre, while the more intimate Mark Taper Forum premieres high-caliber plays. (✆theater 213-628-2772, dance 213-972-0711, opera 213-972-8001; www.musiccenter.org; 135 N Grand Ave; ticket prices vary; **P**; **M**Civic Center)

Orpheum Theater
PERFORMING ARTS

30 ⭐ Map p124, B3

The busiest venue on Broadway is this 1926 theater, built for vaudeville but more recently hosting *American Idol* auditions, concerts and film screenings. (www.laorpheum.com; 842 S Broadway; 🚌MTA 745)

Shopping

Robert Reynolds Gallery GALLERY

31 Map p124, D3

An incredible loft art space owned and operated by the artist himself. He specializes in mixed-media canvasses and sculpture, and uses bamboo, Japanese paper and fiberglass to create fantasy boats and decaying lanterns, and crafts evocative landscapes from nails, straw, grass and wildflowers. Wow! (☏323-599-8485; www.robertreynolds.com; 408 S Spring St; ⊙11am-5pm Mon-Sat; ⓜPershing Square)

Jewelry District JEWELRY

32 Map p124, C3

For bargain bling head to this bustling downtown district where you can snap up watches, gold, silver and gemstones at up to 70% off retail. The mostly traditional designs are unlikely to be seen on the red carpet, but the selection is unquestionably huge. Quality varies, however. Buyer beware. (www.lajd.net; Hill St btwn 6th & 8th Sts; ⓜPershing Square)

Hive GALLERY

33 Map p124, C3

Nestled in a decidedly not-yet-gentrified stretch of Spring St, the Hive is a seemingly small but surprisingly deep artist-owned gallery, where the art always delivers and the openings rock. (www.thehivegallery.com; 729 S Spring St; ⊙1-6pm Wed-Sat; ⎕MTA 28/728)

Last Bookstore in Los Angeles BOOKS

34 Map p124, D3

Operating out of an elegant and expansive lobby space, this used-book and record trader is one of the best of its kind in LA, if not *the* best. The $1 paperbacks are in the foyer, while deep stacks of feminist lit, Beat poetry, pop star biographies, obscure pulp fiction and a few marbled leather classics abut thick granite columns and feel like a literary maze. (www.lastbookstorela.com; 453 S Spring St; ⊙10am-midnight Tue-Wed, to 11pm Thu-Sat, to 6pm Sun; ⓜPershing Square)

Cotrutza Gallery GALLERY

35 Map p124, D3

Cotrutza is a fashionable 50-something Romanian warrior queen with some magnificent politically inspired canvasses, a diorama of poster tubes painted in French-inspired motifs and a wall reserved for guest artists. (www.cotrutza.com; 446 S Main St; ⊙noon-6pm Wed-Fri, 3:30-7:30pm Sat & Sun; ⓜPershing Square)

Virgo VINTAGE

36 Map p124, B3

One of the best shops on the Fashion District fringes. The stock is predominantly vintage 1960s and 1970s gear. Its leather bags and shoes are particularly great. (www.virgoshop.com; 216 E 9th St; ⊙9:30am-6pm Mon-Sat; ⎕MTA 66)

Local Life
Pasadena

Getting There

🚆 **Train** Metrolink's Gold Line serves Pasadena and connects it to downtown.

🚗 **Car** Take I-110 from downtown, or the I-134 from Burbank.

One could argue that there is more blue-blood, meat-eating, robust Americana in Pasadena than in all other LA neighborhoods combined. Here is a community with a preppy old soul, a historical perspective, an appreciation for art and jazz and a slightly progressive undercurrent.

❶ Rose Bowl Stadium & Brookside Park

One of LA's most venerable landmarks, the 1922 **Rose Bowl Stadium** (www.rosebowlstadium.com; 1001 Rose Bowl Dr) can seat up to 93,000 spectators and has its moment in the sun every New Year's Day when it hosts the famous Rose Bowl postseason college football game. It is surrounded by Brookside Park, which is a nice spot for hiking, cycling and picnicking.

❷ Gamble House

It's the exquisite attention to detail that impresses most at the **Gamble House** (www.gamblehouse.org; 4 Westmoreland Pl; adult/student & senior/child free; ☺noon-3pm Thu-Sun; **P**), a 1908 masterpiece of Craftsman architecture built by Charles and Henry Greene for Proctor & Gamble heir David Gamble.

❸ Norton Simon Museum

Rodin's *The Thinker* is only a mind-teasing overture to the full symphony of art in store at this exquisite museum. The highly accessible, user-friendly galleries at **Norton Simon** (www.nortonsimon.org; 411 W Colorado Blvd; adult/senior/child under 18yr & student $10/5/free; ☺noon-6pm Wed, Thu & Sat-Mon, to 9pm Fri; **P**) teem with choice works by Rembrandt, Renoir, Raphael, Van Gogh, Botticelli and Picasso.

❹ Pasadena Museum of California Art

The **Pasadena Museum of California Art** (www.pmcaonline.org; 490 E Union St; adult/student & senior/child $7/5/free; ☺noon-5pm Wed-Sun; **P**) is a progressive gallery dedicated to art, architecture and design created by California artists since 1850. Shows change every few months. The museum is free on the first Friday of every month.

❺ Bistro 45

Touted as the best fine dining in Old Town, the pink-and-green art deco **Bistro 45** (☎626-795-2478; www.bistro45.com; 45 Mentor Ave; mains $20-34; ☺ dinner Tue-Sun; **P**) is elegant yet not stiff. It's the kind of place top Central California winemakers choose if they're hosting a dinner for potential buyers. The seafood, steaks and chops are all seriously good.

❻ Red White & Bluezz

Jazz blows nightly at **Red White & Bluezz** (☎626-792-4441; www.redwhitebluezz.com; 70 S Raymond Ave; ☺10:30am-9pm Sun, from 11am Mon-Wed, 11am-11pm Thu, to midnight Fri & Sat; **P**), so belly up to that fine marble bar and enjoy some of the best LA-area talent doing their thing in intimate, Old Town environs.

Explore

Burbank & Universal City

Home to most of LA's major movie studios – including Warner Bros, Disney and Universal – the sprawling grid of suburbia known as 'the Valley' also has the dubious distinction of being the original world capital of porn, memorably captured in Paul Thomas Anderson's 1997 *Boogie Nights*.

The Sights in a Day

Breakfast at **Bob's Big Boy** (p144), Burbank's original drive-in diner, before heading over to **Warner Bros** (p142) for a working studio tour without the theme park attractions.

Grab lunch among the producers, aspiring writers and actors at **Daichan** (p143), then take the family to **Universal Studios** (p138) for an afternoon and evening of movie-loving adventure. The whole family will enjoy the **Shrek 4-D ride** (p139) and the **Water World show** (p139). If you've had your fill of the theme park disco, blitz over to **It's a Wrap** (p144) before closing time.

If it's a balmy evening and you have tickets for a show at the **Gibson Amphitheatre** (p144), stroll the **Universal Citywalk** (p139). Otherwise, head over to Sushi Row for dinner at the undercover heaven that is **Kazu Sushi** (p142) before letting the night fall around your shoulders at **Firefly** (p144).

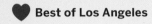

Top Sights

Universal Studios (p138)

Best of Los Angeles

Sushi
Kazu Sushi (p142)

Off-Beat Experiences
Psychic Eye (p144)

Firefly (p144)

NoHo Arts District (p142)

Getting There

Ⓜ **Metro** Universal City is well connected to Hollywood and downtown by the Metro Red Line, while Metrolink connects Burbank with downtown and Long Beach, and the Orange Line heads west into the San Fernando Valley.

Ⓜ **Metro** The most centrally located Red Line stop is Universal City.

Top Sights
Universal Studios

The magic of movie-making gets its due at ever-popular Universal, one of the world's oldest continuously operating movie studios and theme parks, where thrill rides, live performances, inter-active shows and back-lot tram tours perpetually draw the masses. Although it is a working studio, the chances of seeing any action, let alone a star, are slim.

Map p140, E4

www.universalstudios hollywood.com

1000 Universal Center Dr

general admission $77, annual pass $104

⊙vary by season

Ⓜ Metro Red Line

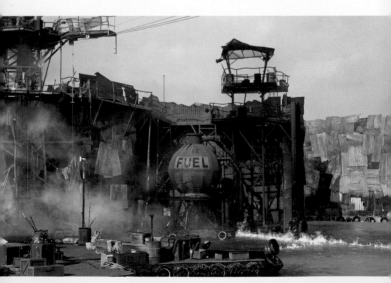

Water World show

Don't Miss

Shrek 4-D Ride

Shrek 4-D takes you from Lord Farquaad's dungeon into a theater where you'll don ogre-vision 3-D glasses and become immersed in the action. You'll head out on an adventure with Shrek's crew that touches all the senses, with moving seats, wind and mist.

Water World Show

The movie may have bombed, but the Water World show is a runaway hit. There are mind-boggling stunts such as giant fireballs and a crash-landing seaplane.

Universal Citywalk

With flashing video screens, oversized facades and garish color combinations, Citywalk hovers beside Universal Studios like a reject from the *Blade Runner*-meets-Willy Wonka school of architecture. Its 65 shops, restaurants and entertainment venues offer a mix of attractions, including the **iFly** (www.iflyhollywood.com) vertical wind tunnel that mimics the feeling of skydiving.

NORMAN WHARTON/ ALAMY®

☑ Top Tips

▶ Try to budget a full day, especially in summer. To beat the crowds, get here before the gates open or invest in the Front of Line Pass ($129) or the deluxe guided VIP Experience ($249).

▶ First-timers should head straight for the 45-minute narrated Studio Tour.

▶ The best thrill ride is Jurassic Park.

✗ Take a Break

▶ There are plenty of dining choices at Universal Citywalk, but we suggest heading to Ventura Blvd's Sushi Row, where you can have sneaky-good affordable fare at Daichan (p143), or deal with the sushi nazi's angry blessings at Sushi Nozawa (p143).

NORTH
HOLLYWOOD

North
Hollywood

Vineland Ave

Chandler Blvd

Weddington St

North
Hollywood
Park

Cahuenga Blvd

Magnolia Blvd

Otsego St

Lankershim Blvd

Hartsook St

NoHo Arts
District

Bakman Ave

Clean Ave

Hollywood Fwy

Riverside Dr

Camarillo St

Ventura Fwy

Moorpark St

Colfax Ave

Tujunga Ave

Riverside Dr

Lankershim Blvd

Arch Dr

Universal
City

Ventura Blvd

Sunshine Tce

Cahuenga Blvd W

Universal

Laurel Canyon Blvd

STUDIO
CITY

0   1 km
0   0.5 miles

E

F

G

H

Clybourn Ave

N Parish Pl

N Keystone St

MAGNOLIA PARK

10

1

W Magnolia Blvd

N Frederic St

N Naomi St

N Florence St

N Catalina St

N Niagara St

Verdugo Park

W Verdugo Ave

Clark Ave

N Buena Vista St

Addison St

2

N California St

N Avon St

W Olive Ave

W Alameda Ave

N Hollywood Way

Johnny Carson Park

Ventura Fwy

7

Buena Vista Park

3

Riverside Dr

Pass Ave

1 Warner Bros Studio VIP Tour

Forest Lawn Memorial Park & Hollywood Hills

Valley Spring Lane

Toluca Lake

Lakeside Country Club

Forest Lawn Dr

4

Los Angeles River

Universal Studios

Griffith Park

Hollywood Dr

UNIVERSAL CITY

9

Barham Blvd

Cahuenga Peak (1840ft)

5

Hollywood Fwy

Sights

Warner Bros Studio VIP Tour
STUDIO TOUR

1 ⊙ Map p140, G4

This tour offers the most fun and authentic look behind the scenes of a major movie studio. The 2½-hour romp kicks off with a video of WB's greatest film hits (*Rebel Without a Cause, Harry Potter* etc) before a tram whisks you to sound stages, back-lot sets and technical departments, including props, costumes and the paint shop. (☏818-972-8687; www.wbstudiotour. com; 3400 Riverside Dr; 2½hr tour $49, child under 8yr not admitted; ◷8:30am-4pm Mon-Fri, some summer weekends; Ⓟ; ◻MTA 155)

NoHo Arts District
NEIGHBORHOOD

2 ⊙ Map p140, C2

Situated at the end of the Metro Red Line, North Hollywood (NoHo) was

---

Top Tip

Be the Laugh Track

Half the fun of visiting LA is hoping you might see a star, so up the odds with a visit to the set of a prime-time sitcom. Multicamera shows such as *Two and a Half Men* and *The Big Bang Theory* are shot before a live audience. That's you.

To nab tickets, check the website for Audiences Unlimited at www.tvtickets.com; to see what's taping, call ☏818-753-3470, or stop by the booth at Universal Studios (p138). For information on tickets for *The Tonight Show with Jay Leno* at NBC Studios, log on to www.nbc.com/the-tonight-show/tickets.

---

a down-on-its-heels neighborhood of artists, but thanks to a redevelopment it now boasts some 20 stage theaters in 1 sq mile and a burgeoning community of galleries, restaurants and vintage clothing stores around them. (www.nohoartsdistrict.com; ⓂNorth Hollywood)

Eating

Kazu Sushi
JAPANESE $$$

3 ✕ Map p140, B5

Stuck in a cramped and otherwise nondescript mini-mall is one of the best-kept secrets among LA's sushi aficionados. It's Michelin rated, very high-end, has a terrific sake selection and is absolutely worth the splurge.

Understand

Car Culture Begins Here

Nobody is suggesting you should blame Burbank for things like smog, gridlock and global warming, but you can blame it for the mini-mall. In fact, Burbank proudly claims to be the inventor of not just the ubiquitous park and shop strips that dominate American suburbia, but also the drive-in movie theater, the drive-through restaurant and the drive-in bank.

It's a Wrap (p144)

(818-763-4836; 11440 Ventura Blvd; meals from $50; lunch Mon-Fri, dinner Mon-Sat; P ; MTA 150/240)

Daichan JAPANESE $$

4 Map p140, C4

Stuffed with knickknacks, pasted with posters and staffed by a sunny and sweet owner-operator, this offbeat Japanese diner offers the best (and one of the tastiest) deals on Sushi Row. Order the Negitoro bowl, in which fatty tuna is served over rice, lettuce and seaweed. (11288 Ventura Blvd; mains $8.25-16; lunch & dinner Mon-Sat; P ; MTA 150/240)

Sushi Nozawa JAPANESE $$$

What would Sushi Row be if it didn't have an honest-to-goodness sushi

nazi? You know, the kind who tells you what you'll eat and does not tolerate the slightest insurrection. Just sit quietly at Sushi Nozawa, near Daichan (see 4 Map p140, C4), and munch gratefully. (818-508-7017; www. sushinozawa.com; 11288 Ventura Blvd; meals from $35; lunch & dinner Mon-Fri; P ; MTA 150/240)

Asanebo SUSHI $$$

5 Map p140, A4

Asanebo is a Michelin-star standout thanks to dishes such as halibut sashimi with fresh truffle, and *kan-pachi* with miso and serrano chilies. (818-760-3348; 11941 Ventura Blvd, Studio City; dishes $3-21; lunch Tue-Fri, dinner Tue-Sun; MTA 150/240)

Artisan Cheese Gallery CHEESE $$

6 Map p140, A4

You don't have to be a cheese head to enjoy a meal here, but it sure helps. Inside are woodblocks stacked with wheels and wedges of the stinky stuff. You can get platters and staff will pair them with wine and beer for you, or you could opt for a gourmet sandwich. (www.artisancheesegallery.com; 12023 Ventura Blvd; salads & sandwiches $8.75-13; ⊙10:30am-7pm Mon-Thu, to 9pm Fri & Sat, 9:30am-5pm Sun; P; MTA 150/240)

Bob's Big Boy AMERICAN $

7 Map p140, F3

The red-checkered, pompadoured kid still woos hamburger-craving hordes at America's oldest remaining Big Boy. Grab a burnt-orange booth inside, or enjoy carhop service on weekend nights. (www.bigboy.com; 4211 Riverside Dr; ⊙24hr; 📶; MTA 155)

Drinking

Firefly LOUNGE

8 Map p140, A4

Firefly has the sexiest library this side of an Anne Rice novel – bordello-red lighting, low-slung couches and flickering candles, all surrounded by shelves of somber-looking tomes. Not that anyone's opened one. The members of this upwardly mobile crowd are too busy reading each other. (www.fireflystudiocity.com; 11720 Ventura Blvd, Studio City; ⊙5pm-2am; MTA 150/240)

Entertainment

Gibson Amphitheatre LIVE MUSIC

9 Map p140, F5

This is a major indoor venue for headlining pop acts. Lately it's also been bringing in some of the biggest names in Latin pop. (www.livenation.com; 100 Universal City Plaza; MUniversal City)

Shopping

It's a Wrap CLOTHING

10 Map p140, F1

This packed-to-the-rafters store sells clothing worn by cast members from TV and film. Persistence pays – from J Crew and Laura Ashley to Bebe and Juicy, the racks hold treasures galore. New arrivals are racked by show affiliation. (📞818-567-7366; www.itsawraphollywood.com; 3315 W Magnolia Blvd; ⊙10am-8pm Mon-Fri, 11am-6pm Sat & Sun; MTA 183)

Psychic Eye NEW AGE, OCCULT

11 Map p140, A4

West of Burbank in Sherman Oaks, this longtime pipeline of psychics and astrologers, amulets and idols, is a third eye–opener. If there's a spell you'd like to cast or break, if you need intuitive advice or would otherwise like to peer into the past or the future, find this strange vortex of the occult. (📞818-906-8263; www.pebooks.com; 13435 Ventura Blvd; readings 15/30/60min $20/30/50; ⊙10am-10pm Mon-Sat, to 8pm Sun; P; MTA 150/240)

Understand

The 'Industry'

From the moment film – and later TV – became the dominant entertainment medium, LA took center stage in the world of popular culture. It's also been the best (and sometimes the worst) ambassador of LA to the world. You might know it as entertainment, but to Angelenos it's simply the 'Industry.'

Entrepreneurial moviemakers – most of them European immigrants – established studios here in the first decade of the 20th century. German-born Carl Laemmle built Universal Studios in 1915, selling lunch to curious guests coming to watch the magic of movie-making; Polish immigrant Samuel Goldwyn joined with Cecil B DeMille to form Paramount Studios; and Jack Warner and his brothers arrived a few years later from Poland via Philadelphia. Perpetually sunny weather meant that most outdoor locations could be easily shot, and movie-making flourished.

Fans loved early film stars such as Charlie Chaplin and Harold Lloyd, and the first big Hollywood wedding occurred in 1920, when Douglas Fairbanks wed Mary Pickford. What's more, the proximity of the Mexican border enabled filmmakers to rush their equipment to safety when challenged by the collection agents of patent holders such as Thomas Edison.

Although Hollywood became the cultural and financial hub of the movie industry, only Paramount Pictures is in Hollywood proper. Studios were built in Culver City (MGM, now Sony Pictures), Studio City (Universal Studios Hollywood) and Burbank (Disney and Warner Bros). The first big movie palaces were not on Hollywood Blvd but on Broadway in downtown LA.

Although LA sometimes feels like a company town, like Washington, DC for government or – at one time – Detroit for automobiles, the Los Angeles Economic Development Council reported that in 2009 only some 154,000 people in LA County were employed directly in film, TV and radio production. That doesn't tell the whole story, though, because the Industry churns more jobs, from high-powered attorneys to cater-waiters. Still, the region's economic reach is much more than making pretty pictures.

All that aside, for stargazers and movie buffs, LA is the equivalent of the Holy Grail.

Top Sights
Disneyland & Disney California Adventure

Getting There

🚗 **Car** Anaheim is 25 miles southeast of downtown LA on 1-5, exit Disneyland Dr.

🚆 **Train** Orange County line from Union Station to Anaheim Station; then transfer to Anaheim Resort Transit 15.

Mickey is one lucky mouse. Created by animator Walt Disney in 1928, this irrepressible rodent is a multimedia juggernaut, and he lives in the 'Happiest Place on Earth.' The land of Disney is a slice of 'imagineered' hyper-reality, where the streets are always clean, the park employees – called cast members – are always upbeat, and there's a parade every day of the year. Even cynics must admit that since opening his home to guests in 1955, he's been a pretty thoughtful host to millions of blissed-out visitors.

Treasure Room, Pirates of the Caribbean attraction

Don't Miss

Tomorrowland

To the right of the plaza is Tomorrowland, a vision of what imagineers back in the 1950s thought the future might look like – monorails, rockets and Googie-like architecture, it seems. Today, most of the attractions have been updated, and the biggest thrills come from *Star Wars*–inspired **Star Tours**, with its buffeting Star-Speeder rocketing through a big-screen, slightly nauseating deep space. **Space Mountain**, with its tight turns, screaming drops and blaring music, remains one of the park's most adrenaline-filled attractions. **Finding Nemo's Submarine Voyage** is an upcycled Disneyland classic.

Fantasyland

Classic stories and characters dwell in Fantasyland, where the canal ride through multilingual versions of 'it's a small world' still charms. For a surprisingly irreverent little trip, hop aboard **Mr Toad's Wild Ride**, inspired by *The Wind in the Willows,* for a loopy jaunt through Mr Toad's mansion, underground London, Winky's Pub and, sadly, the courthouse.

Frontierland, New Orleans Square & Adventureland

The **Big Thunder Mountain Railroad** roller coaster awaits in Frontierland, where pioneers, miners and Tom Sawyer live on. New Orleans Sq houses the spooky, but not too scary, **Haunted Mansion** as well as the ever-popular 16-minute **Pirates of the Caribbean** boat ride. Yes, the ride was here first! **Indiana Jones** beckons from Adventureland with a lurching drive in an oversized jeep through an archaeologist's worst nightmare, or is it really his own twisted fantasy?

http://disneyland.
disney.go.com

1313 S Disneyland Dr

adult & child over 10yr $80, child 3-9yr $74, park-hopper tickets $105/99

🕙10am-8pm Mon-Thu, 8am-midnight Fri & Sat, 8am-11pm Sun

☑ Top Tips

▶ Stay overnight for maximum exposure. Try **Disneyland Hotel** (☎714-778-6600; 1150 Magic Way) or the stunning **Disney's Grand Californian Hotel** (☎714-635-2300; 1600 S Disneyland Dr).

▶ Stop at free FASTPASS kiosks with your ticket, and you'll be assigned an hour-long time frame to enjoy an attraction. With it, you can cut to the front of the line.

▶ On Main St there's a parade every evening.

✕ Take a Break

Ready for a break from big-eared mice and boysenberry pie? Try Little Saigon in Westminster, 7 miles southwest of Anaheim.

Twilight Zone Tower of Terror

The big attraction of Disney California Adventure's **Hollywood Pictures Backlot**, if not the entire park, is the Twilight Zone Tower of Terror, a 13-story drop down an elevator chute situated in a haunted hotel – eerily resembling the historic Hollywood Roosevelt Hotel in Los Angeles.

From the upper floors of the tower, you'll have views of the Santa Ana Mountains, if only for a few heart-pounding seconds.

Golden State

Golden State is the adrenaline-addled sector of Disney California Adventure. Its main attraction, **Soarin' over California**, is a virtual hang-gliding ride using Omnimax technology that lets you float over landmarks such as the Golden Gate Bridge, Yosemite Falls, Lake Tahoe, Malibu and, of course, Disneyland itself. Enjoy the light breeze as you soar, keeping your nostrils open for the smell of the sea, orange groves and pine forests blowing in the wind.

Grizzly River Run takes you 'rafting' down a faux Sierra Nevada river – you will get wet, so come when it's warm. While fake flat-hatted park rangers look on, kids can tackle the **Redwood Creek Challenge Trail**, with its 'Big Sir' redwoods, wooden towers and lookouts, and rock slide and climbing traverses.

Ariel's Undersea Adventure & Cars Land

Part of the Disney California Adventure revamp, these new additions are sure to captivate fans of Pixar and Disney classics alike. The recently unveiled Ariel's Undersea Adventure, patterned after Disneyland's Haunted Mansion ride, begins in a Victorian mansion where you'll hop aboard a clamshell that will transport you through underwater scenes of the classic film. All the stars – Ariel, Prince Eric, Sebastian and Flounder – will be there to greet you.

Based on the Pixar franchise, Cars Land is more than a ride, it's an entire new section of the park, complete with rides, shopping and dining options. You can glide through the air aboard **Luigi's Flying Tires**, and race through 6 acres of red-rock landscapes and reach speeds of up to 40mph aboard **Radiator Springs Racers**.

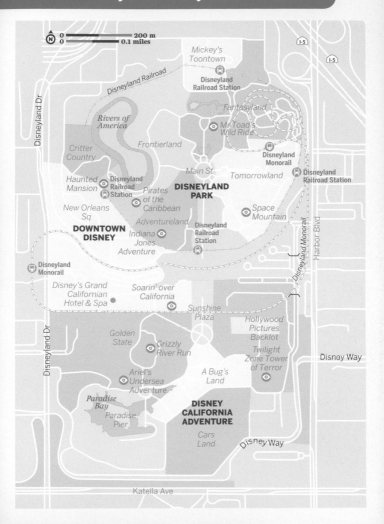

The Best of
Los Angeles

Manhattan Beach (p114) pier
RICHARD CUMMINS/LONELY PLANET IMAGES ©

Best Walks
The Venice Stroll

🏃 The Walk

Step into the Venice lifestyle and rub shoulders with folks who believe that certain truths will only be revealed to those who disco-skate in a Speedo and turban ensemble. And, while such people may exist largely in their own universe, they happen to know that there are more moments of Zen packed into this tiny beach community than in most other 'hoods combined.

Start Ocean Front Walk and Washington Blvd; 🚌BBB 1

Finish Abbot Kinney Blvd; 🚌MTA 33

Length 3.5 miles; two hours

🍴 Take a Break

The best place to put your feet up is one of the many cafes and restaurants along Abbot Kinney Blvd. If you're hungry for a quick bite, consider GTA (p107) or Abbot's Pizza Co (p108), or tuck into something more substantial at Joe's (p107).

❶ South Venice Beach

South of the Venice Pier is the untrammeled beach of South Venice.

❷ Venice Canals

Even many Angelenos have no idea that just a couple of blocks away from the boardwalk madness is an idyllic neighborhood that preserves 3 miles of canals of the famed developer and tobacco mogul Abbot Kinney.

❸ Venice Boardwalk

The famed **Venice Boardwalk** (p104) is a vortex for the loony, the free-spirited, the hip and athletic. Here are outdoor gyms, beach rentals, skate parks and drum circles.

❹ Muscle Beach

Gym rats with an exhibitionist streak can get a tan and a workout at this famous **outdoor gym** (p105) right on the Venice Boardwalk where Arnold once bulked up alfresco.

Venice Beach

❺ Venice Beach Graffiti Park

Keep your camera at the ready as you approach the tagged-up towers and freestanding concrete wall of **Venice Beach Graffiti Park** (p105), forever open to aerosol Picassos to curb vandalism.

❻ Venice Beach Skate Park

Long the destination of local skate punks, the concrete at **Venice Beach Skate Park** (p105) has now been molded and steel-fringed into 17,000 sq ft of vert, tranny and street terrain with unbroken ocean views.

❼ Fig Tree's Café

If you're hungry already, **Fig Tree's Café** (p110) serves the best eats on the boardwalk.

❽ Ballerina Clown & the Chiat/Day Buildings

On Main St are two of Venice's more captivating buildings. The **ballerina clown** (p108) rises like a twisted god/goddess from the corner of Main and Rose on an other-wise pedestrian building. Across the street is Gehry's epic **Chiat/Day** (p108) building.

❾ Abbot Kinney Boulevard

Abbot Kinney, the man who dug the canals and christened the town, would probably be delighted to find the stretch of his name-sake **boulevard** (p107) stacked with unique, individually owned boutiques, galleries and sensational restaurants.

Best Walks
The Downtown Hustle

🏃 The Walk

Downtown is the most historical, multilayered and fascinating part of Los Angeles. There's great architecture, from 19th-century beaux arts to futuristic Frank Gehry. There's world-class music at the Walt Disney Concert Hall, top-notch art at the Museum of Contemporary Art (MOCA), superb dining and a Fashion District. You'll see it all as you explore this power nexus, creative vortex and ethnic mosaic.

Start LA Live; M Pico

Finish Union Station; M Union Station

Length 3.8 miles; three hours

🍽 Take a Break

When you're doing the Downtown Hustle there are but two reasons to pause. The Grand Central Market (p126) is a byzantine wholesale market with fun food stalls, and then there's Philippe the Original (p129), where the French dip was invented.

Pershing Square

❶ The Grammy Museum

Easily the highlight of LA Live is the **Grammy Museum** (p126). Music lovers will get lost in interactive exhibits that define, differentiate and link musical genres, while live footage strobes from all corners.

❷ Fashion District

The axis of the **Fashion District** (p122), this 90-block nirvana for shopaholics is the intersection of 9th and Los Angeles Sts, where fashionistas and designers congregate.

❸ Broadway Theater District

Highlighted by the still-running Orpheum Theatre, built in 1926, **Broadway** (p126) was LA's entertainment hub with no fewer than a dozen theaters built in a riot of styles.

❹ Pershing Square

The hub of downtown's historic core, Pershing Sq was LA's first public park, and is now enlivened by public art and summer concerts.

❺ Grand Central Market

On the ground floor of the 1905 beaux arts **Grand Central Market** (p126) is where architect Frank Lloyd Wright once kept an office.

❻ Museum of Contemporary Art

The **Museum of Contemporary Art** (p126), housed in a building by Arata Isozaki, has a collection that arcs from the 1940s and includes works by Mark Rothko and Dan Flavin.

❼ Walt Disney Concert Hall

A molten blend of steel, music and psychedelic architecture, Gehry pulled out all the stops for the iconic **Walt Disney Concert Hall** (p120).

❽ Pueblo de Los Angeles

Here's where LA's first colonists settled in 1781. **Pueblo de Los Angeles** (p127) preserves the city's oldest buildings.

❾ Union Station

A glamorous Mission Revival achievement with art deco accents, **Union Station** (p126) opened in 1939 as America's last grand rail station. Bukowski worked at the historic Terminal Annex post office just north of the station.

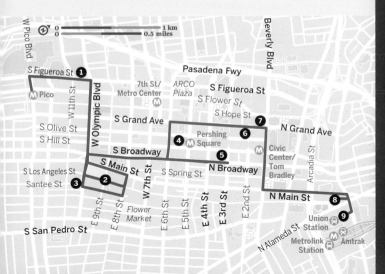

Best
Food

When one considers the great eating towns of the world, Los Angeles is often overlooked. Yet, it is here that celebrity chefs such as Nobu Matsuhisa and Wolfgang Puck rose to stardom, where market fresh health food first morphed into cuisine, and where the diversity of culture and community converge into some of the best ethnic kitchens in the USA.

The Big Shots

OK, so somewhere along the way chefs became celebrities, and the kitchen became a stage, and that arguably all started in Beverly Hills with Wolfgang Puck and Spago in the 1980s. It's also true that ever since then the world's best chefs have flocked to these celebrified streets to serve power lunches and dinners, and bask in the glow of Hollywood stars, and then partner with them. These days, chefs such as the aforementioned Matsuhisa, Thomas Keller, Mario Batali and Michael Voltaggio are among the culinary celebs ready to serve you.

Well Fed

For years after anxious Alvie Singer met a perturbed Annie Hall for an awful health-food meal at the end of Woody's iconic film, LA had been synonymous with tasteless, unsatisfying health food. But then something incredible happened. Wheat germ and flax seed were sublimated and health-minded chefs started getting way-out creative.

These days, LA is saturated in farmers markets, market cafes and enough meatless joints to make even the most militant veg-head shed an alkaline tear of joy. Even omnivores will love that raw vegan ice-cream they scoop at Sage.

BRENT WINEBRENNER/LONELY PLANET IMAGES ©

☑ Top Tips

▶ Check Pulitzer Prize winner Jonathan Gold's weekly 'Counter Intelligence' column in the *LA Weekly* for more off the beaten ethnic kitchens and gourmet prose.

▶ LA restaurants fill up between 7pm and 9pm, but if you don't mind dining late, arrive after 9pm and you won't wait long for a table.

CHRISTINA LEASE/LONELY PLANET IMAGES ©

Best Market Cafes

Joan's on Third (p80)

Forage (p48)

Huckleberry (p94)

Lemonade (p109)

Best Celeb Kitchens

Pizzeria Mozza (p79)

Ink (p61)

Matsuhisa (p81)

Bouchon (p59)

Best Ethnic Eateries

Sushi Ike (p29)

Yakitoriya (p60)

Yuca's (p48)

Jitlada (p29)

Kazu Sushi (p142)

Best Vegan Vortex

Flore (p48)

Seed (p108)

Sage & Kind Kreme (p53)

Real Food Daily (p95)

Ethnic Pride

The pride we speak of is not simply the kind inherent in any proud, culturally awake and aware chef poised to share his or her tradition with their ravenous public. It's the kind of pride that Angelenos often feel when they've tasted flavors that explode in new directions, when the food they eat tells some other kind of story that gets their mind bounding around the world. And it's the pride in sharing their discovery over a long, wine-drenched meal with family and friends.

Best
Drinking

DAVID PEEVERS/LONELY PLANET IMAGES ©

Dry and dusty LA may be, but you will not go thirsty. After all, this is the town of Lebowski and Bukowski, and where Kiefer Sutherland and Gary Oldman's legendary long lunch led to Oldman's DWI arrest in the wee small hours. LA is where Slash discovered Jack Daniels, and where some of America's most creative bartenders mix and muddle craftsman cocktails with a smirk or a smile.

Cracked Ice

Some time around 2007 the US got swept up in a speakeasy undertow. It started in the East Village then sprouted in San Francisco, which means LA was the third major metropolitan area to fall in love with cracked-ice, jazz-age cocktails. Could it have been an omen of a stratified economy, swollen credit figures and forthcoming economic doom? Who really cares? Just order another round and try not to think about it.

Simple & Straight

Some of us prefer not to have complexities such as pomegranate or grapefruit juice; simple syrup and freshly snipped herbs get in the way of a fine spirit. Does this mean we lack taste? It simply suggests that when we go out drinking, we seek establishments that serve only the best rums, tequilas, mescals, whiskeys and bourbons distilled from this sweet earth, and when we finally arrive at the bar, we peruse the selection, order something generally high end, usually aged, and always neat.

☑ Top Tips

▶ To minimize mortal injury to yourself and others, get to know an LA niche by strategically sampling bars within walking distance of one another. Cab it back to the hotel and do it all over again tomorrow.

▶ Downtown offers countless hip and tasty scenes within a short stroll.

Cat & Fiddle

Best Muddlers

Copa d'Oro (p97)

Comme Ca (p61)

Roger Room (p82)

Association (p130)

Best Hard Stuff

La Descarga (p31)

El Carmen (p82)

Las Perlas (p130)

Harvard & Stone (p32)

Best Wine & Beer Bars

Good (p49)

Venice Beach Wines (p110)

Oscar's Cerveteca (p109)

Best Dives

Galley (p96)

Thirsty Crow (p49)

Cat & Fiddle (p31)

To Wine or Not to Wine

Sometimes it's best to pretend that there is no such thing as hard liquor, and instead relax into the time-tested comforts of a great bottle of burgundy. Or perhaps you crave something crisp, dry and Californian, or something cold and frosty devised by Belgian monks or Colorado hipsters or German beer-gineers. Rest assured, there are beaucoup LA bars and pubs eager to cater to grape lovers and barley devotees alike.

Best **Museums**

Museums grand and austere, sprawling and magical, tucked away and hidden in plain sight, are dotted all across the Greater Los Angeles Area. Here are Shinto shrines, there's a window into 'Jurassic technology', in the middle of town there's a revamped neo-classic that is also a part-time jazz hub, to the right of it are prehistoric remains, and way up there is a mega-monster of a museum masterwork that is stuffed with so many of Getty's goodies it's almost unfathomable. If you're not feeling culturally aware, awake or relevant in LA, you won't be alone, but it will be your own fault.

☑ **Top Tips**

► Most if not all of LA-area museums offer specific 'free days' to their public. Some are free all day once a week, or once or twice monthly, and still others offer a few hours free a week.

Best Museums

Getty Center (p68)

LACMA (p74)

MOCA (p126 and p58)

Getty Villa (p101)

Museum of the American West
(pictured right; p47)

Best Alternate Realities

Museum of Jurassic Technology (p87)

Jadis (p94)

Santa Monica Museum of Art (p93)

Wall Project (p78)

Best
Live Music

Live music should be considered a natural resource. Like nature, its presence affects moods and circumstance; it can also inspire new creativity, technology and economies. It's a nourishing flow that can fertilize the seeds of catharsis, loosen the intellect and enliven the spirit.

DAVID PEEVERS/LONELY PLANET IMAGES ©

Night Music

Just like the perfect set of waves, or that first spring rain you can never be quite sure when, or if, it will happen, you do know that if your fellows are open of mind, and the musicians of the moment are generous of heart, that there will be the possibility of greatness; of feeling new and alive in the Southern California night. Of course, the first step is finding your way to the music, and in LA that is absurdly easy. It's not quite New Orleans – where free live music is a birthright, but there's no shortage of venues or musical styling here, either. This, after all, was home to a robust record industry before the digital age, and it remains abundant in musical minds.

Whether they be the hippie rockers and electro-mixologists of Echo Park, or the jazz cats of LACMA, whether they belong to the local philharmonic or are simply blasting through town and exploding on legendary stages like the global pop virtuosos they have become, there will be night music in Angel City. Always.

Best Stages
Hollywood Bowl (p32)
Greek Theatre (p50)
House of Blues (p63)
Music Box (p33)
Echo & Echoplex (p52)

Best Free Concert Venues
LACMA (p74)
California Plaza (p128)
Getty Center (p68)
Santa Monica Pier (p90)
Bardot (p34)

Best
Shopping

There's no other way to really say it. Angelenos are compulsive shoppers. Yes, there are more ways to spend money in this sugary, sun-dappled town than there are ways to make it. There are more purchasing options at the local newsstand than at most small-town grocers. Seriously, you can buy anything here. A human skull? Check. A three-speed vibrator with multiple attachments? Check. A vintage, turn-of-the-century, Parisian baby doll dress? Check. Japan-imation action figures for grown-up hipsters? Yes! Not to mention some of the best and worst fashion hits to come out of any workshop at any point in human history.

High End, Darling

Heavyweight fashion houses cluster around Melrose Pl, and Fred Segal has two such outposts. Just know that if you do enter these hallowed halls, you will want to buy everything, compulsively seek out ever more obscene price tags in a blind 'but-I-want-these!' rage and you may whimper, even as you fork over a week's pay for a pair of stockings or some eyeliner. But, hey, this is LA, baby. There's no crying at the register!

Keep it Indie

Here's the one knock on the indie shops, labels and boutiques: they're all so damn expensive when compared to the Banana Republics of the world. But if you're into shopping with honor, and espouse a 'first, do no harm' lifestyle, then you will seek out LA's indie boutiques. You might make a sample sale in the Fashion District, and hunt down start-up designers on the Silver Lake streets.

RAY LASKOWITZ/LONELY PLANET IMAGES ©

☑ Top Tips

▶ Save gas and traffic-induced aggravation by conquering LA-area boutiques a neighborhood at a time. That way you can walk off that long/liquid lunch as you stroll, browse and buy, buy, buy!

▶ LA's farmers markets are not just great places to brunch and people-watch – often young, indie designers set up stalls and offer tasty boho wear and elegant jewelry.

TED SOQUI/CORBIS ©

Best of the Snooty Set

Barneys New York (p67)

Diane von Furstenberg (p67)

Fred Segal (p66 and p99)

Best Weird Stuff

Spitfire Girl (p50)

Pleasure Chest (p66)

Necromance (p67)

Wacko (p51)

Munky King (p67)

Best Rummage

Fashion District sample sales (p122)

Melrose Trading Post (p66)

It's a Wrap (p144)

House of Quirk (& Smut)

If you are partial to midnight screenings of the *Rocky Horror Picture Show*, and enjoy the strange microtastes of all-over-the-map gift shops, then LA is your Neverland.

There's more strange on offer here than any place other than NYC. And, yes, that includes long-running and well-regarded sex shops, too.

Best
Kids

Looking around Rodeo Dr, Sunset Strip and downtown's Grand Ave, it's easy to think that LA's children have been banished to a gingerbread cottage in the woods. But the kids are here.

DAVID PEEVERS/LONELY PLANET IMAGES ©

Get to Know the Nodes

The term in city planning these days is 'nodes' (art nodes, shopping nodes) – islands of specificity dotting the urban landscape. Kid-friendly nodes include the beaches, where crafty parents can wear out their tykes with bike-riding and body-surfing, as well as LA's parks, where hiking, exploring and animal-watching are top notch.

Young *Animal Planet* devotees can ogle humanesque chimps at Griffith Park's LA Zoo, while future paleontologists can study skeletal sabre-toothed cats pulled from the La Brea Tar Pits (p72). And, of course, don't forget the kiddiest nodes of all, theme parks, with options ranging from all-day happiness at Disneyland (p146) and Universal Studios (p138) to momentary thrills at Pacific Park (p91). And if you don't have kids, feel free to avoid aforementioned nodes at all costs.

Best Kid-Friendly Museums

Griffith Observatory (p42)

Museum of the American West (p47)

Best Kid-Friendly Restaurants

Uncle Bill's Pancake House (p115)

Abbot's Pizza Co (p108)

Farmers Market at 3rd and Fairfax (p81)

Best Animal-Watching

LA Zoo (p46)

Griffith Park (p47)

Roundhouse Aquarium (p115)

Best Outdoor Fun

LA Zoo (p46)

Griffith Park (p47)

Manhattan Beach (p114)

Santa Monica Pier and Beach (p90)

Best
Gay & Lesbian
Los Angeles

RICHARD I'ANSON/LONELY PLANET IMAGES ©

LA is one of the country's gayest cities. Your gay-dar may well be pinging throughout the county, but the rainbow flag flies especially proudly in Boystown, along Santa Monica Blvd in West Hollywood (WeHo), flanked by dozens of high-energy bars, cafes, restaurants, gyms and clubs. Most cater to gay men, but there's plenty for lesbians and mixed audiences. Thursday to Sunday nights are prime.

Scoping the Scene

Beauty reigns supreme among the buff, bronzed and styled of Boystown. Elsewhere, the scene is more laid-back and less body-conscious. The crowd in Silver Lake runs from cute hipsters to leather-and-Levi's bears and an older contingent. Venice and Long Beach have the most relaxed, neighborly scenes.

Except for the hardcore places, LA's gay spots get their share of opposite-sex and straight patrons, drawn by gay friends, the fabulousness of the venues, abundant eye candy and, for women in gay bars, a non-threatening atmosphere.

The Arts

There's gay theater all over town, but the **Celebration Theatre** (www.celebrationtheatre.com; 7051 Santa Monica Blvd, West Hollywood) ranks among the nation's leading stages for LGBT plays. West Hollywood's annual October 31 Halloween Carnival draws a crowd of 500,000 to Santa Monica Blvd. June's LA Gay Pride parade and festival (www.lapride.org) is a celebration of diversity that draws huge crowds to the neighborhood with exhibits and shows.

The annual AIDS walk draws thousands of fundraisers to the starting line at the Pacific Design Center (p58) for the 6.2-mile trek.

Best Nightspots
Abbey (p62)

Palms (p62)

Factory/Ultra Suede Gay (p65)

Best Day Spots
Runyon Canyon (p58)

Hugo's (p60)

Book Soup (p65)

Fred Segal (p66, p99)

Café Stella (p47)

Best **Outdoor Adventure**

RUSS BISHOP/ALAMY ©

With bike paths, mountain trails, pounding surf and wind-blown seas minutes away, the question isn't whether you should enjoy the outdoors, but how? Possibilities for adventure are almost endless; just ask the parade of bikers, surfers and boat owners hustling past for their daily outdoor fix.

Get Physical

Hollywood visitors short on time can zip a loop around Runyon Canyon northwest of La Brea Ave, where a steep uphill climb, great views and a no-leash policy lures Hollywood hipsters and their pooches. Griffith Park boasts 53 miles of trails plus the iconic hike to the summit of Mt Hollywood (*not* the location of the sign), where stellar 360-degree views await, smog-willing. Tree-lined trails along the coastal mountains give it up for ocean and canyon fans, while bikers bounce over the Backbone Trail on the southern spine of the Santa Monicas. Beach cruisers may prefer the flat 22-mile South Bay Bicycle Trail from Santa Monica to within a spoke of Palos Verdes.

Don't like exercising alone? John Muir's 110-year-old Sierra Club lets non-members join its organized, very welcoming hikes and bike rides, geared to various fitness levels. See www.angeles. sierraclub.org to choose from hundreds. The night hikes are especially cool. Mountain-bikers should check www.corbamtb.com and www.socalmtb.com for conditions.

Best Short Hikes with Views

Coldwater Canyon to Fryman Canyon (p39)

Hollyridge Trail (p43)

Runyon Canyon (p39)

Best Ease-of-Access Biking

South Bay Bicycle Trail (p91)

Griffith Park (p47)

Best
Beaches

The stars of *Baywatch, The OC* and *Laguna Beach* weren't the first photogenic faces to inspire waves of California dreamin'. Nope, that would be George Freeth – one part Irish, one part Hawaiian and one part Victorian surf god – who arrived on LA's shores 100 years ago with a wooden surfboard to promote Hawaiian tourism. But tycoon and local booster Henry Huntington persuaded young George to stick around, paying him to surf in front of his hotel. Tourists and locals were hooked, and California surf culture was born.

Beach Life at its Best

Today, surfers head to Malibu's Surfrider beach, while South Bay wave hounds check out Manhattan Beach. But it's not all about the perfect break. Santa Monica's wide sandy swath is perfect for quintessential beach living – volleyball, bodysurfing and sunbathing are top-notch. Same goes for Manhattan and the beach south of the Venice Pier, where the crowds are lighter.

For rambling, El Matador and Westward Beach near Point Dume offer nature-minded opportunities galore. That's where the seals, sea lions and dolphins play and breach for lucky beachcombers. If you encounter beachside fencing, unleash your inner libertarian and defy them! According to California law, all beaches are public.

STEPHEN SAKS/LONELY PLANET IMAGES ©

Best People-Watching

Venice Boardwalk (p104)

Manhattan Beach (p114)

Santa Monica Beach (p90)

Best for Beachcombing

El Matador (p101)

Westward Beach (p101)

Surfrider (p101)

Best
Celebrity-
Spotting

Admit it. You want to see a celeb. Of course you do. You're in Hollywood. So don't apologize for it. Prophets, poets, professional actors – people are drawn to a famous face. Maybe it's the talent we love, or feeling connected to the world through one anointed person, or thinking we'll absorb a bit of the holy glow. Or maybe they're just hot or cool, or... hot.

Getting Your Star Fix

The University of Southern California published a study finding that actors tend to be more narcissistic than the rest of society. Uh, yeah, and too much cheese is fattening. That said, it suggests that fan-love sates their needs as well as your own.

So, how to fulfill two needs with one gawk? Driving past stars' homes is a start, but it's unlikely you'll see anyone. As for velvet-rope clubs, you may not get in and the doorman might hurt your feelings. So where to look for stars? In their natural habitat, of course. Restaurants are primo, especially in Hollywood, West Hollywood and Mid-City. Those with patios and hidden nooks are best. As for cinemas, spotting celebs at the ArcLight is a good bet. Shopping works, too. Stores can't survive on Lindsay and Britney alone, so browse their faves on Robertson Blvd and Abbot Kinney Blvd. Finally, hillside trails are favored for exercise. Who was that jogging past in the baseball cap?

MARIANNA MASSEY/CORBIS ©

Best Cinemas for Star Sightings

ArcLight (p33)

Pacific Theatres at the Grove (p84)

Popular Celeb Shopping Spots

Fred Segal (p66, p99)

Kitson (p66)

Abbot Kinney Boulevard (p107)

Celeb Sighting Almost Guaranteed

Runyon Canyon (p39)

Bar Marmont (at Chateau Marmont, pictured above; p61)

Warner Bros Studio VIP Tour (p142)

Best Celebrity-Spotting Restaurants

Joan's on Third (p80)

Dan Tana's (p59)

AOC (p80)

Campanile (p80)

Ita Cho (p79)

Survival Guide

Survival Guide

Before You Go

When to Go

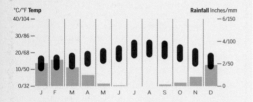

°C/°F Temp
40/104 —
30/86 —
20/68 —
10/50 —
0/32 —

J F M A M J J A S O N D

Rainfall Inches/mm
— 6/150
— 4/100
— 2/50
— 0

➡ **Spring (Apr-Jun)** Wildflowers bloom in the hills, rain is scarce and the sun shines warm on southern California.

➡ **Summer (Jul-Sep)** Inland temperatures begin to soar and air quality suffers, but by the sea overcast skies (aka June Gloom) can persist through July.

➡ **Autumn (Oct-Dec)** The first of LA's two short wet seasons begins in October. But between storms temperatures stay in the 70s and the skies are blue.

➡ **Winter (Jan-Mar)** The more significant rainy season; it's also when mountains appear snow-glazed beyond downtown, and wildflowers bloom.

Book Your Stay

When choosing overnight digs in Los Angeles, the primo decision is location. Staying at a posh Santa Monica beach hotel is probably not the best choice if you're catching a performance at Walt Disney Concert Hall downtown or visiting Universal Studios in Burbank. It can be done, but your happiness quotient will rise or fall depending how long you're sitting in your car. That said, most neighborhoods have hotels in just about every price range, though expect to pay between $130 and $200 per night for a midrange room.

Useful Websites

Los Angeles Hotel Accommodations (www.losangeleshotelaccommodations.com) A local discount online booking site.

Trip Advisor (www.tripadvisor.com) User-generated reviews and booking service.

Orbitz (www.orbitz.com) It offers discounted rates, but always cross-check with the hotel's own website to be sure.

Best Budget

Stay (www.stayonmain.com) A hip hostel in the heart of downtown and set on the first two floors of a historic hotel.

Hotel Cecil (www.stayon main.com) The host hotel of the Stay Hostel. This is a great second choice if the hostel fills up.

Elaine's Hollywood Bed & Breakfast (www.elaines hollywoodbedandbreakfast. com) This B&B offers four rooms in a lovingly restored 1910 bungalow.

Best Midrange

Hotel Figueroa (www. figueroahotel.com) It's hard not to be charmed by this rambling owner-operated oasis with chic decor.

Standard Hollywood (www.standardhotel.com) This Sunset Strip haunt has you shacking up in sizable shagadelic rooms that wink at the 1960s.

Avalon Hotel (www. avalonbeverlyhills.com) Mid-century modern gets a 21st-century spin at this fashion-crowd fave, which was Marilyn Monroe's old pad in its days as an apartment building.

Best Top End

Hollywood Roosevelt (www.hollywoodroosevelt. com) Often the place to be for poolside parties. The cabanas are the way to go if you're looking to splurge.

The London (www.thelon donwesthollywood.com) A sleek, grand all-suite property on the doorstep of the Sunset Strip.

Hotel Bel Air (www.hotel belair.com) Recently redone and one of LA's iconic properties, this classy Spanish colonial estate is favored by royalty – Hollywood and otherwise.

Arriving in Los Angeles

Air

Los Angeles International Airport (LAX; ☏310-646-5252; www.lawa. org/lax) is about 17 miles southwest of downtown, bounded by the Pacific Ocean to the west and the San Diego Fwy (I-405) to the east.

There are nine terminals in the U-shaped complex, including the Tom Bradley international terminal located at the base of the U. The terminals are accessible by car on two levels, the upper used for departures and the lower for arrivals.

Foreign currency exchange and ATMs are found in every terminal. Hotel and car-rental information kiosks are located in or adjacent to baggage claim.

A **first-aid station** (☏310-215-6000; ⏰10am-10pm) can be found on the south side of the upper level of the international terminal. In case of an emergency, call **airport police** (☏310-646-7911).

Terminal maps are available at www.lawa.org.

Midsized LA airports include Burbank's **Bob Hope Airport** (BUR; ☏818-840-8840; www.burbankairport.com) and **Long Beach Airport** (LGB; ☏562-570-2600; www. longbeach.gov/airport).

Train

Amtrak (☏800-872-7245; www.amtrak.com), America's national rail service, rolls into downtown Los Angeles at historic **Union Station** (800 N Alameda St).

Bus

Greyhound (☎800-231-2222; www.greyhound.com) operates extensive, if slow, routes across North America. Its main Los Angeles terminal is **downtown** (☎213-629-8401; 1716 E 7th St).

Travel Passes

The **Metro Transit Authority** (☎800-266-6883, TTY 800-252-9040; www.metro.net) operates about 200 bus lines as well as seven Metro Rail lines. Introduced in 2009, a plastic, rechargeable **Transit Access Pass** (TAP; www.tapgo.net) can be used throughout the county in addition to cash. Currently, the MTA sells weekly ($20) passes, valid on both bus and rail lines. Tickets and passes are sold at more than 400 retail outlets around town, and at MTA customer centers including **Union Station** (◷6am-6:30pm Mon-Fri) and **Mid-City** (5301 Wilshire Blvd; ◷9am-5pm Mon-Fri).

Getting Around

In this book, the nearest metro station or bus route is noted with the reviews. Although having a car is preferable, if you confine your excursions to the Hollywood–Los Feliz–downtown swirl you can do just fine with the Metro Red Line. And it's only a moderate ride from West Hollywood and Beverly Hills to Santa Monica aboard buses equipped with bike racks. Bring a bicycle and your mobility and possibilities expand.

Bus

A network of bus routes spans the metropolis, with most operated by **Metro Transit Authority** (MTA; ☎800-266-6883, TTD 800-252-9040; www.metro. net). Its one-way fare starts at $1.50 and goes up to $2.90 for freeway routes. Most routes operate 5am to 2am daily.

Transportation Within LA

	Burbank	Downtown	Hollywood
Burbank		Metro red line 20min	Metro red line 4min
Downtown	Metro red line 20min		Metro red line 15min
Hollywood	Metro red line 4min	Metro red line 15min	
LAX	car 1hr	Flyaway shuttle 45min-1hr	car 45min-1hr
Long Beach	car 1hr-90min	Metro blue line 53min	car 90min
Pasadena	car 30min	Metro gold line 25min	car 35-45min
Santa Monica	car 1hr	Big Blue Bus 10 40-90min	car 45min-1hr

Individual tickets (exact fare required) can be purchased from the bus driver.

Fast, frequent Metro Rapid buses (numbered in the 700s) make limited stops. Bus 720 travels downtown from Santa Monica via Westwood, Beverly Hills and Mid-City's Miracle Mile along Wilshire in about 45 to 90 minutes, depending on departure time.

Big Blue Bus

Santa Monica's **Big Blue Bus** (☎310-451-5444; www. bigbluebus.com) rumbles through much of western LA including Beverly Hills, Culver City, Westwood/ UCLA and Venice. One-way fares are $1 and transfers to a different bus or bus system are 50¢. The freeway express

to downtown LA costs $2 (from another bus, transfer is $1). Big Blue Bus routes are abbreviated 'BBB' in this book's reviews.

Metro Rail

Operated by MTA, Metro subway and light-rail trains connect downtown with Hollywood, Los Feliz and Universal City (Red Line), Pasadena (Gold Line), LAX (Green Line), Long Beach (Blue Line) and Korea Town (Purple Line). One-way fares are $1.50. Trains run approximately 5am to midnight.

Taxi

Most companies charge a $2.85 base fee then $2.70 per mile. Don't expect to hail a cab from the sidewalk; you need to call ahead.

Try **Beverly Hills Cab Co** (☎800-273-6611), **Checker Cab** (☎800-300-5007) or **Taxi Taxi** (☎310-444-4444, SM pick-up only). Costs can add up quickly in traffic-snarled LA. Surcharges for airport drop-offs, pick-ups and extra passengers and luggage may also apply.

Car & Motorcycle

If you're planning to visit several neighborhoods, it may be wise to rent a car. Because of LA's sprawl, public transportation can be cumbersome and time-consuming, while taxis can be prohibitively expensive.

Rental rates start at about $35 a day or from $125 a week for unlimited mileage, exclusive of taxes and insurance. Secure a low price via

	LAX	Long Beach	Pasadena	Santa Monica
LAX		car 1hr-90min	car 30min	car 1hr
	Flyaway shuttle 45min-1hr	Metro blue line 53min	Metro gold line 25min	Big Blue Bus 10 40-90min
Long Beach	car 45min-1hr	car 90min	car 35-45min	car 45min-1hr
Pasadena		car 45min	car 40min-1hr	car 20-30min
Santa Monica	car 45min		car 45min	car 45min
	car 40min-1hr	car 45min		car 40min
	car 20-30min	car 45min	car 40min	

the internet or phone in advance, usually with no cancellation penalty.

LA's freeways are variously referred to by number or by name. To add to the fun, the same freeway may have a different name in a different region. Here are the biggies:

I-5 Golden State/Santa Ana Fwy

I-10 Santa Monica/San Bernardino Fwy

I-110 Pasadena/ Harbor Fwy

I-405 San Diego Fwy

I-710 Long Beach Fwy

US 101 Hollywood/ Ventura Fwy

Hwy 1 Pacific Coast Hwy (PCH)

Freeways should be avoided during rush hour (5am to 9am and 3pm to 7pm), although traffic jams can occur at any time. Beachfront highways get jammed on weekend mornings, and Sunset Strip is slow going on weekend nights.

On-street parking can be tight. If you find a spot, it may be metered or restricted, so obey posted signs to avoid a ticket. Private lots and

parking garages cost at least $5 a day and can be much more expensive downtown. Valet parking at hotels can cost as much as $30 a day.

Municipal lots near Rodeo Dr in Beverly Hills and bordering Third St Promenade in Santa Monica are free for two hours.

Driver's License

Visitors can legally drive in California with a valid driver's license issued in their home country. An International Driving Permit is not compulsory.

Essential Information

Business Hours

Normal business hours are 9am to 5pm Monday to Friday. Banks usually open from 8:30am to 4:30pm Monday to Thursday and to 5:30pm on Friday; some also open from 9am to 2pm on Saturday.

Post offices are open from 9am to 6pm weekdays, and some also open 9am to 2pm on Saturday.

Shops open from 10am to 7pm Monday to Saturday, though shopping malls may close later, and open from 11am to 6pm on Sunday.

Bars are generally open from late afternoon until 2am.

Restaurants generally serve lunch from 11am to 3pm and dinner from 5:30pm to 10pm.

Electricity

120v/60hz

120v/60hz

Emergency

Police, fire, ambulance
(📞911)

Police (nonemergency)
(📞877-275-5273)

Rape & Battery Hotline
(📞800-656-4673)

**Rape Treatment Center,
UCLA** (📞310-319-4503)

Holidays

New Year's Day January 1

**Martin Luther King Jr
Day** Third Monday in
January

Presidents' Day Third
Monday in February

Easter A Friday and Sunday in March or April

Memorial Day Last
Monday in May

Independence Day July 4

Labor Day First Monday
in September

Columbus Day Second
Monday in October

Veterans' Day
November 11

Thanksgiving Fourth
Thursday in November

Christmas Day
December 25

Safe Travel

Traffic accidents are your
biggest threat in Los
Angeles, so make sure
to buckle up, even in a
taxi. It's actually the law
in California. Take care
not to drink and drive;
designate a driver.

As in most big cities,
it's wise to keep your wits
about you late at night,
particularly in unfamiliar
or poorly lit areas.

Violent crime is mostly
confined to well-defined
areas of East LA and
South LA, as well as less-
trafficked blocks in Hol-
lywood, Venice and down-
town. Avoid these areas
after dark. Downtown is
the site of 'Skid Row,' an
area roughly bounded
by 3rd, Alameda, 7th and
Main, where many of the

city's homeless spend
the night.

During earthquakes,
stand under a sturdy
doorframe and protect
your head with your arms
until tremors subside.

Tipping

Bars 15%; minimum tip
$1 per order

Hotel porters $1 to $2
per item

Restaurants 15% to
20%; tip may be included
as a 'service charge' on
bill for large groups

Taxis 10% to 15%

Valet parking $2

Telephone

US cell phones operate
on GSM 1900. If your
home country uses a
different standard, you'll
need a multiband GSM
phone to make calls in
LA. If you have an un-
locked multiband phone,
a prepaid rechargeable
SIM chip is usually cheaper than using your own
network. You can also
buy inexpensive prepaid
phones.

City Codes

All California phone num-
bers consist of a three-
digit area code followed

by a seven-digit local number. Even local calls from cell phones require the entire number to be dialed. Toll-free numbers start with ☑800, ☑866, ☑877 or ☑888.

Anaheim (☑657, 714)

Beverly Hills, Culver City, Malibu, Santa Monica, South Bay (☑310, 424)

Burbank (☑747, 818)

Echo Park & Downtown LA (☑213)

Hollywood, Los Feliz, Mid-City, Silver Lake (☑323)

Pasadena & San Gabriel Valley (☑626)

Useful Phone Numbers

Country code (☑1)

International direct dial tone (☑011)

International operator (☑00)

Local directory inquiries (☑411)

Operator (☑0)

Toll-free directory inquiries (☑1-800-555-1212)

Toilets

Most supermarkets and all restaurants and bars allow customers to use their facilities. Smaller

shops don't tend to offer the privilege.

Tourist Information

The main tourist offices:

Downtown Los Angeles Visitor Information Center (Map p124, D2; ☑213-689-8822; 685 S Figueroa; ☺8:30am-5pm Mon-Fri) Between 7th St and Wilshire.

Hollywood Visitor Information Center (Map p26, C3; ☑323-467-6412; cnr Hollywood & Highland, 6801 Hollywood Blvd; ☑10am-10pm Mon-Sat, to 7pm Sun)

Los Angeles Convention & Visitors Bureau (☑213-624-7300, 800-228-2452; www.lacvb.com) Provides maps, brochures and lodging information plus tickets to theme parks and attractions.

Other tourist offices:

Beverly Hills Conference & Visitors Bureau (☑310-248-1015, 800-345-2210; www.beverlyhillsbehere.com; 239 S Beverly Dr; ☺8:30am-5pm Mon-Fri)

Pasadena Convention & Visitors Bureau (☑626-795-9311, 800-307-7977; www.pasadenacal.com; 300 E

Green St; ☺8am-5pm Mon-Fri, 10am-4pm Sat)

Santa Monica Visitor Information Kiosk (Map p92, A2; Palisades Park, 1400 Ocean Ave; ☺9am-4pm winter, to 5pm summer)

Santa Monica Visitors Center (Map p92, B4; ☑310-393-7593, 800-544-5319; www.santamonica.com; 1920 Main St, Suite B; ☺9am-6pm)

West Hollywood Convention & Visitors Bureau (Map p56, D3; ☑310-289-2525; www.visitwesthollywood.com; 8687 Melrose Ave, Suite M38, inside Pacific Design Center; ☺8am-6pm Mon-Fri)

Travelers with Disabilities

Under current law, public buildings, restrooms and transportation (buses, trains and taxis) are required to be wheelchair accessible. Larger hotels and motels have rooms designed for guests with a disability.

For paratransit and door-to-door services, contact **Access Services Incorporated** (☑800-827-0829; www.asila.org). Check with individual car rental agencies for hand-controlled vehicles or vans with wheelchair lifts. **Wheelers** (☎800-456-1371; www.wheelersvanrentals.com) specialize in these vehicles. You must have a permit for parking at blue-colored curbs and specially designated spots in public lots.

If you need assistance in LA, contact **LA County Commission on Disabilities** (☎213-974-1053, TTY 213-974-1707; www.laccod.org). On its website, the **Society for Accessible Travel & Hospitality** (SATH; ☎212-447-7284; www.sath.org) provides links to numerous sources of information about traveling with a disability.

Visas

Since the rules for entry into the US are constantly changing, check with the United States Consulate in your home country for up-to-date information as well as the visa website of the US Department of State (www.unitedstatesvisas.gov; www.travel.state.gov/visa) and the travel section of US Customs & Border Protection (www.cbp.gov).

Under the US Visa Waiver programs (VWP), visas are currently not required for citizens of 36 countries for stays of up to 90 days (no extensions allowed) provided they have a machine-readable passport (MRP). If you don't have an MRP, you'll need a visa and a passport valid for six months after the date of your expected stay, and your trip must be for business or tourism.

VWP travelers must have an approved Electronic System for Travel Authorization (ESTA). To apply, register online with the Department of Homeland Security at http://esta.cbp.dhs.gov at least 72 hours before visiting. Registration is generally valid for two years or until your passport expires.

Citizens from all non-visa-waiver countries need to apply for a visa in their home country. The process may take some time, so apply as early as possible.

Behind the Scenes

Send Us Your Feedback

We love to hear from travelers – your comments help make our books better. We read every word, and we guarantee that your feedback goes straight to the authors. Visit **lonelyplanet.com/contact** to submit your updates and suggestions.

Note: We may edit, reproduce and incorporate your comments in Lonely Planet products such as guidebooks, websites and digital products, so let us know if you don't want your comments reproduced or your name acknowledged. For a copy of our privacy policy visit lonelyplanet.com/privacy.

Our Readers

Many thanks to the travelers who used the last edition and wrote to us with helpful hints, useful advice and interesting anecdotes: Ilona Bicker, Ashlea Lewis.

Adam's Thanks

Thanks to Dan Cohn (the man knows where to eat), Jon Regardie at Downtown News, Eddie Lin, Trisha Cole, Guru Singh, Burton Breznick, Paul Feinstein at Party Earth, Chris Sorensen and Adria Heath, Sam, Andrew, Suki and the entire Lonely Planet squad, and to the sweet and gorgeous Georgiana Johnson.

Acknowledgments

Cover photograph: Manhattan Beach pier, Go Places/Alamy. Many of the images in this guide are available for licensing from Lonely Planet Images: www.lonelyplanetimages.com.

This Book

This 3rd edition of *Pocket Los Angeles* was written by Adam Skolnick. Andrew Bender contributed some of the text. The previous edition (*Los Angeles Encounter 2*) was researched and written by Amy C Balfour. This guidebook was commissioned in Lonely Planet's Oakland office, and produced by the following:

Commissioning Editor Suki Gear **Coordinating Editors** Carolyn Boicos, Rebecca Chau **Coordinating Cartographer** Julie Dodkins **Coordinating Layout Designer** Jacqui Saunders **Managing Editor** Anna Metcalfe **Senior Editor** Susan Paterson **Managing Cartographer** Alison Lyall **Managing Layout Designer** Jane Hart **Assisting Editors** Alice Barker, Justin Flynn, Kate James **Assisting Layout Designers** Yvonne Bischofberger, Mazzy Prinsep **Cover Research** Naomi Parker **Internal Image Research** Sabrina Dalbesio **Thanks to** Lucy Birchley, Janine Eberle, Ryan Evans, Victoria Harrison, Liz Heynes, Laura Jane, David Kemp, Karyn Noble, Trent Paton, Piers Pickard, Kirsten Rawlings, Lachlan Ross, Michael Ruff, Julie Sheridan, Laura Stansfeld, John Taufa, Angela Tinson, Gerard Walker, Clifton Wilkinson

Index

See also separate subindexes for:

⊗ **Eating p181**

⊙ **Drinking p182**

✿ **Entertainment p182**

🔒 **Shopping p183**

Our Writer

Adam Skolnick

Adam Skolnick is a third-generation, born-and-raised Los Angeleno whose family moved from the old country to Boyle Heights, the Fairfax District, and finally to Santa Monica over the past century. A freelance journalist, he writes about travel, culture, health, sports and the environment for Lonely Planet, *Men's Health*, *Outside*, *Travel & Leisure* and *Spa*. He has authored and coauthored nine previous Lonely Planet guidebooks and, ahem, a few unsold screenplays. He lives in Santa Monica and Bali, but has an increasing fondness for downtown and Echo Park. You can read more of his work at www.adamskolnick.com. His new web series, *Aspiring*, is online at www.youtube.com/user/theholdingpattern.

Published by Lonely Planet Publications Pty Ltd
ABN 36 005 607 983
3rd edition – May 2012
ISBN 978 1 7417 9826 5
© Lonely Planet 2012   Photographs © as indicated 2012
10 9 8 7 6 5 4 3 2 1
Printed in China